CRACKING THE DA VINCI CODE

Simon Cox is the editor-in-chief of
Phenomena, the magazine devoted to
challenging dogmas, orthodoxies and
half-truths. He has also worked as a
researcher for some of the leading
names in the alternative history field,
including Robert Bauval, David Rohl
and Graham Hancock. Simon is
currently making a TV documentary
based on the facts behind
The Da Vinci Code for a major US
production company.

CRACKING THE DA VINCI CODE

The Unauthorized Guide
to the Facts
Behind Dan Brown's
Bestselling Novel

SIMON COX

Sterling Publishing Co., Inc.
New York

This edition published by Sterling Publishing Co., Inc.
by arrangement with Michael O'Mara Books Ltd

10 9 8 7 6 5 4 3 2 1

Published in 2004 by Sterling Publishing Co., Inc.
387 Park Avenue South, New York, NY 10016

First published in Great Britain in 2004 by
Michael O'Mara Books Ltd

Every effort has been made to trace and contact copyright holders of all
materials in this book. The author and publishers will be glad to rectify
any omissions at the earliest opportunity.

For more facts behind the fiction, visit www.crackingdavinci.com

Designed and typeset by Design 23

Distributed in Canada by Sterling Publishing
c/o Canadian Manda Group
One Atlantic Avenue, Suite 105
Toronto, Ontario, Canada M6K 3E7

Library of Congress Cataloging-in-Publication Data Available

1-4027-1837-3

Printed and bound in the United States of America by
Quebecor World, Martinsburg, WV

Terribilis est locus ist

Inscription found at the entrance to the
church at Rennes-le-Château

CONTENTS

Acknowledgments

All books are team efforts; don't let anyone tell you any different. The team effort involved with this labor was a brilliant one, and I would like to offer my absolute thanks as I call out the roll of honor.

It seems appropriate that I have my own group of goddesses to thank first and foremost. For the brilliant research by one of the world's best, I would like to thank Jacqueline Harvey—dinner is on me. For the extra material, my thanks are to Robin Crookshank (no hyphen) Hilton. SPD, you were brilliant. No words can describe my thanks adequately.

Chaps there were, too, who helped a great deal. Mark Foster, for the artwork and the photo manipulation—where have all the people gone? Mark Oxbrow for Rosslyn—Templars? What Templars? Geoff Petch for the calls and the encouragement. Andy Gough for the list and great conversation. Jim Chalmers whose idea it was in the first place.

My thanks also go out to my friends and family—Mum, Dad, Mark, and Claire. Gemma Smith for the gee up and the kick up the butt, Sam for being good at last.

Lindsay Davies at Michael O'Mara for the commission and the coffee—next time can I have a bit longer to finish, please? Robert Kirby at PFD—the world's most patient literary agent—now lunch is on me.

Introduction

Considering the context of the Holy Grail, it is not surprising that the subject has polarized opinion for many years. Even so, it is rare for a novel to cause as much controversy as *The Da Vinci Code*. As this book goes to press, the figures for worldwide sales of Dan Brown's murder mystery are racing toward the six million mark, with sales set to go even higher on the release of the paperback version. There doesn't seem to be any middle ground in the reaction to the book—people either love it or hate it, a fact that makes the book the more extraordinary.

Let's take the detractors first. These are generally divided into certain subgroups. First, there are those who consider Brown's book to be historically inaccurate and poorly researched. Then there are those who see in Brown's novel a major challenge to Christian dogma and orthodoxy. It's not too hard to see why, when one flicks through the pages of *The Da Vinci Code*, its main premise being that the Christian Church has been hiding something from us all for two millennia. Powerful stuff indeed, and strong enough to draw venomous attacks from fundamentalists, apologetics, and Christian liberals alike. A quick flick through some pages on the Internet will show you that Brown has raised the ire of more than one Christian scholar, with page upon page being dedicated to "breaking" his novel and its adjudged attack on the Christian faith. Indeed, some of these selfsame Christian apologists are bringing into print their own books, denouncing Brown's novel as a sham and a heinous crime against God-fearing folk the world over.

These arguments are based around Brown's retelling of the idea, drawn from various books in the alternative history genre, that Jesus was married to Mary Magdalene, who bore their child and so promulgated a family line through history. Such a notion seriously questions the concept of Christ's divinity, as this hypothesis would make him a "flesh and blood" man rather than the Son of God. I discuss the bloodline thesis at length in the Mary Magdalene section of this book, so will not go over the main argument here. What I will say, however, is that taken at absolute face value, and using the Gospels and Scriptures of the New Testament as our guide, the apologists are quite correct in their counter-claims that there is no direct evidence for such a union between Christ and the Magdalene. However, what they haven't addressed with their reading of the Scriptures and Gospels is one of the central themes of this hypothesis: namely, that this information was deemed so damaging and disruptive to the early Church that it was actually suppressed by the original redactors and editors of the New Testament—being, in effect, written out of the original texts, to be replaced by a sanitized version that was much more appealing to the early Church Fathers. If you are looking for a denouncement of Brown and his novel, you have come to the wrong place—there are other books that will interest you more. This book is aimed squarely at the first subsection of detractors and at those who love the novel but are a little puzzled about the history and factual evidence behind the book. I have tackled these issues head-on in the following pages.

Dan Brown undoubtedly drew on a small handful of books for his main themes and background material. For the general idea that there exists a bloodline of Christ and that this was through the union of Jesus and Mary Magdalene, along with the theory that a secret society known as the Priory of Sion exists to keep this arcane secret safe, Brown has used the controversial best-seller, *Holy Blood, Holy Grail*, by Michael Baigent, Henry Lincoln, and Richard Leigh, as his basis. For the idea that Leonardo Da Vinci encoded some of these themes and secrets into his paintings, he has turned to *The Templar Revelation*, by Lynn Picknett and Clive Prince, and for his material on Mary Magdalene and the Sacred Feminine he has used *The Woman with the Alabaster Jar*, by Margaret Starbird. Those who have read *The Da Vinci Code* will be familiar with the fact that these three books adorn the bookshelf of the fictional Grail scholar, Leigh Teabing, at his home, Château Villette. The books are named, but their authors are not. In *The Da Vinci Code*, Brown only scratches the surface of some of the theories put forward in the above books; to fully understand the depth of research and argument posited, it would be well worth reading at least one of the books cited above and included in the bibliography at the end of this book.

If there is indeed a bloodline from Christ, then we are faced with what we can loosely call two heresies: a small heresy and a larger, more fundamental, heresy. The small heresy is a simple one: the Church has lied for 2,000 years, hiding the truth from Christians for various reasons. The larger heresy is huge. For if this theory is proved correct, then whole swathes of history have to be rewritten and, with them, our very understanding of the fabric of life, faith, and the world around us. There is much at stake.

So why is *The Da Vinci Code* so popular? First and foremost, it's a good story. The book reads well, and no doubt it will make a great movie, under the directorship of Ron Howard. I also think there is a deeper reason for its success. What Dan Brown has touched is a raw nerve in much of his readership. Many people are unhappy with the way they have been taught to think and believe, and a desire to break out of the box and dig deeper into life's mysteries is gaining momentum as we settle into the twenty-first century. It's this raw nerve that *The Da Vinci Code* has jumped on. I seriously doubt that the book is compelling thousands of Christians to question their faith and abandon the Church. What it is doing, however, is bringing into the mainstream a river of thought and a host of theories that have until now been seen as alternative and in some way heretical. Surely this is a good thing.

This book is designed in such a way as to give the reader of *The Da Vinci Code* a primer on many of the factual elements in the book. It is set out in a simple A to Z format and is, I hope, easy to navigate and read. I have endeavored to keep the entries as brief as necessary in order to avoid the feel of an academic textbook, or indeed to bore the reader. What I hope I have achieved is an awakening in the reader of a realization that there is real mystery and strangeness in the historical world. I hope I have encouraged at least some to read further and to dig deeper—in this I am sure that Leonardo would have approved.

Adoration of the Magi

"Everyone loves a conspiracy." So Dan Brown prefaces his snippet of information concerning the Leonardo unfinished masterpiece, *Adoration of the Magi*. In *The Da Vinci Code*, Brown, through his narrative, retells the story of how a Florence-based art diagnostician (a modern-day art archaeologist, one might say) called Maurizio Seracini had found that layers of grime and overpainting actually covered a very different composition by Leonardo and that the Uffizi Gallery in Florence, embarrassed by these findings, had "banished" the painting to a nearby warehouse. For this information, Brown has his characters quote from a *New York Times Magazine* article titled "The Leonardo Cover-Up."

The *New York Times Magazine* article referred to was indeed real, written in April 2002 by Melinda Henneberger. The article highlighted the work of Maurizio Seracini, who is a real Florence-based art diagnostician. Seracini has become famous for his use of ostensibly medical technology to reveal the secrets of the old masters. His work has encompassed the paintings of Botticelli, Caravaggio, and Raphael as well as many other great master painters. The Uffizi Gallery, where the *Adoration of the Magi* resides, asked Seracini to examine the painting and resolve the debate raging in the art world: should the masterpiece be subjected to restoration, as *The Last Supper* has in recent years? Many believed that the painting was in too fragile a condition to be subjected to the rigors of restoration, and others, principally the head of the Uffizi, countered that the painting was suffering after years of neglect and badly needed, at the very least, a good cleanup.

Seracini came to some remarkable and controversial conclusions about the painting, conclusions that are still to be fully appreciated and accepted by the art world. In Seracini's words, "None of the paint we see on the *Adoration* today was put there by Leonardo. God knows who did, but it was not Leonardo." Seracini believes that a much later hand was responsible for the clumsily applied layer of brown and orange paint that now adorns the painting. He points out that many of the painted features are totally devoid of the finesse and quality of Leonardo's hand, especially in the way parts of the human anatomy are depicted. Not only that, but Seracini has found evidence that beneath the layers of paint and grime a wholly different scene awaits the viewer from the one that was later painted in.

So far, *The Da Vinci Code* is correct in what it has to say about the *Adoration of the Magi*; however, there is more. Dan Brown seems to intimate that the Uffizi took the painting down after Seracini's discoveries about the masterpiece. This is not the case. The painting was removed to a warehouse while undergoing the scans that Seracini carried out and while the directors of the Uffizi decided on the appropriate action to take. A notice was indeed put up in room number 15 at the Uffizi, the Leonardo gallery, saying that the picture had been removed for restoration, common practice in these circumstances. The findings of Seracini are difficult ones for both the gallery and for many in the art world who have for years ascribed the painted portions of the work to Leonardo. The idea that there is a conspiracy to hide the real "meaning" of the painting from the general public is perhaps pushing things a little far.

However, it is clear that the work of Seracini has revealed much that was previously hidden under the paint. The images beneath the layers of paint and varnish were glimpsed at by the use of infrared reflectography. These images show a scene quite different from the general theme now seen in the painting. It seems that Leonardo wanted to portray a world that was being reconstructed from ruins, a reflection of the master's feelings at the beginning of the Renaissance. This theme can be glimpsed by the figures that are building a staircase in the original version. Another area of the original painting shows several horses joined in a violent clash, making this scene an early version of Da Vinci's legendary *Battle of Anghiari*, and showing that Leonardo had mastered the movement and expression of intense emotion that the later painting was said to have. Seracini is currently engaged in a search for the fabled *Battle of Anghiari*, which was said to have been painted on one of the walls of the Hall of 500 in the Palazzo Vecchio in Florence. He is convinced that the painting could still exist behind one of the walls of the great hall.

The *Adoration of the Magi* was commissioned in 1481. It is a large painting—96 by 97 inches—and painted on some 10 wooden boards that are glued together. It has been considered a work of genius, and until Seracini's recent work was held in high regard because of its contrasting use of paint and sketched figures. It shows a scene, now fading, of the three kings visiting the infant Jesus and His mother Mary. There are some interesting and possibly symbolic elements to the picture that *The Da Vinci Code* does not highlight. In the painting, there appears to be a carob tree behind the central scene and gathering of people. As Clive Prince and Lynn Picknett point out in their book *The Templar Revelation*, the carob was a tree associated with John the Baptist, a central figure in many of Leonardo's paintings. Around this tree in the painting, a second set of people is gathered, seemingly paying homage to the tree itself, one of them raising the index finger of his left hand in what Prince and Picknett call the John gesture. A second figure in the crowd around the Virgin and Child is also raising his finger, a gesture that Leonardo used many times in his works. The John gesture remains one of the most enigmatic and mysterious elements of Leonardo's body of work.

See also: Leonardo Da Vinci.

Albigensian Crusade

One of the anti-heretical Crusades, carried out by the Christian Church in the thirteenth century against the Cathars, also known as Albigensians after the Cathar stronghold of Albi, a town in the Languedoc, France. The story of the Cathars is central to the themes raised in *The Da Vinci Code*. The main 'secret' at the heart of the novel—the theory that Jesus and Mary Magdalene were married—is a Cathar belief. It is the Church's suppression of these heretical theroies that forms the basis of Dan Brown's plot.

The Albigensian Crusade was a particularly bloody and ruthless Crusade, and it is estimated that from 1209, when it was started, to 1255 over 100,000 Cathars and Languedocians had been massacred. The campaigns were chronicled by the Cistercian monk Pierre des Vaux-de-Cernay in his book *Historia Albigensis*.

In the Languedoc, the Cathars' influence and authority were seriously undermining the Catholic Church. Pope Innocent III was particularly concerned and exasperated by the attitude of the Languedocian nobility, who did little to prevent the Cathars from practicing their faith or to deal with their growing threat. In 1206, Count Raymond VI of Toulouse refused to join a league of knights that the Papal legate, Abbot Arnaud Amaury, had sought to form in order to rid the region of Cathars. Raymond VI had no wish to wage a war against his own subjects, and in May 1207 he was therefore excommunicated at the behest of Amaury's assistant, Pierre de Castelnau. In January 1208, while visiting Raymond VI, Castelnau was murdered by one of the count's knights. This blatant attack on the Papal authority infuriated Innocent III to such an extent that he called for a Crusade against Languedoc, and the Cathars in particular. The call was taken up by the northern barons, probably tempted by the wealth of the Languedoc and the Papal authority to take

Cathar lands with impunity. One such knight was Simon de Montfort, who played an integral role in the Albigensian Crusade and whose name spread fear and hatred into the inhabitants of the region.

The first major casualty of the Crusade was the town of Béziers, which de Montfort's forces reached on July 21, 1209. The Crusaders ordered the Catholic townspeople to hand over the Cathars living among them, but they refused. They were then told they could leave the town without fear so that the Crusaders could enter it and arrest the Cathars. If they failed to do so, the townspeople were threatened with excommunication—a real and forceful deterrent at that time. Despite this warning, the townspeople refused to leave the Cathars and even swore an oath to defend them. The forces of de Montfort, therefore, besieged the town, with Amaury, the Papal legate, telling them to "show no mercy neither to order, nor to age, nor to sex. Cathar or Catholic, kill them all. God will know His own." The ensuing massacre resulted in the slaughter of approximately 15,000 men, women, and children, of whom only 222 were Cathars.

The next town was Narbonne, which submitted to de Montfort's forces, and by August 1209 Carcassonne also surrendered after a short yet vicious siege, after which the townspeople were allowed to leave taking "only their sins with them." The conquered lands were given to de Montfort, and most of the army was disbanded.

However, in his absence the recently defeated towns and castles aligned with Raymond VI of Toulouse, only to be re-conquered by de Montfort and his allies at a later date. As the Crusade re-commenced, many more towns and castles fell, and by 1213 all the lands of the Trencavel had been conquered and Toulouse captured.

The only power at this time that was capable of defeating the Crusaders belonged to Peter, King of Aragon, who held suzerainty over some lands in France and sought to maintain and increase his influence there. In September 1213, he attacked Muret in Toulouse but was defeated and killed by de Montfort's army. In 1215, de Montfort campaigned along the Dordogne, seizing many abandoned Cathar castles, including Domme and Castelnaudary. At this time, Prince Louis of Spain and his forces joined de Montfort's army at the siege of Toulouse.

From 1215 to 1225, many towns rallied together against the Crusaders, including Avignon, an important town that fell within the Count of Provence's domain. In 1216, the garrison town of Beaucaire saw de Montfort's first major defeat, but his forces regrouped and were able to go on to capture Toulouse and Bigerre, being defeated at Lourdes, the western limit of the Albigensian Crusade.

In September 1217, Raymond VII, with help from Aragon, took Toulouse. In the spring of the following year, de Montfort besieged the town but was killed on June 25, 1218, by a stone fired from an artillery engine that was being operated by a group of women. With the loss of de Montfort, the Crusade took on a different outlook from this point on as there was no longer a man of his abilities and energy to lead the Crusaders. The lack of a coherent leader allowed Raymond VII and the Count of Foix to defeat the French at Bazière. Much of the Midi region was now in the hands of Raymond VII and his allies. The triumphs of Raymond VII led to a resurgence of Catharism, and by 1224 the status quo was such that little had been gained by the Crusaders and the position was similar to how it had been in 1209.

In 1226, Louis VIII of France led a new Crusade into the Languedoc, with the majority of towns and castles surrendering without a fight, a sign of the battle-weariness of the population. However, Avignon held out for three months before surrendering on September 12, 1226. On King Louis

VIII's death in Auvergne on November 8, 1226, his seneschal, Humbert de Beaujeu, conducted the Crusade, besieging Labécéde, where he slaughtered the whole population. The last bastion of resistance was Toulouse, which endured a harsh siege. This ended only when it was agreed that the daughter of Raymond VII would marry the son of Blanche de Castille. On April 12, 1229, Raymond VII agreed to the terms of the Treaty of Paris, agreeing also to fight the Cathar heresy, demolish the defenses of Toulouse, obey the Church, and pay damages of 20,000 marks. It is at this point that the Inquisition was established in Toulouse, and from 1233 within the whole of Languedoc. All Cathars were hunted down, tortured, and burned. The horrific activities of the Inquisition caused great unrest within the region, causing revolts at Toulouse, Cordes, Albi, and Narbonne. In 1240, Raymond-Roger IV of Trencavel led a final revolt at Carcassonne but was defeated and left France with his army.

The persecution of the Cathars led most to flee to the few remaining Cathar fortresses, the most famous being Montségur in the Pyrenees, a strongly fortified fortress perched atop a steep mountain. The siege began in November 1243, and by February 1244 the people within finally surrendered. On March 16, the 210 Cathars within Montségur marched down the mountain and were burned as heretics in a field below. In August 1255, the siege of Quéribus, a small Cathar fortress, marked the end of the Albigensian Crusade.

See also: Cathars.

Ankh

The ankh is the ancient Egyptian symbol and hieroglyph meaning "life." Depicted as a looped cross, it is thought to represent a sandal strap or penis sheath. Most Egyptologists believe it to be the former, because of the importance of wearing sandals in Egypt, bearing in mind that death by treading barefoot on a scorpion was a very real danger. However, some have theorized that the ankh may in fact represent the reproductive organs of the female, which would make logical sense, given its life-giving qualities. This association with the female or goddess is why Jacques Saunière, curator at the Louvre in *The Da Vinci Code*, has added a large number of ankhs to the museum collection.

The life-giving quality of the ankh was closely associated with the king as depicted in ancient Egyptian temple scenes. This was especially emphasized in the reliefs of the Amarna period, where the sun's many rays end in ankh symbols that are offered to the noses of the pharaoh Akhenaten and his wife Nefertiti. The offering to the royal nostrils was called the "breath of life."

As the ancient Egyptians believed that the written word was so powerful and mysterious it could bring objects to life, individual signs were considered to have their own divine potency. Because of the nature and intrinsic power of the sign, the ankh became a common magical icon used widely as a protective amulet. When color was added to the ankh symbol, protective energy could be summoned up for the wearer. Thus, a red ankh would denote life and regeneration, blue would indicate fertility, green was connected to healing, white was for ritual purity and was therefore used for ritual ankh objects, and black indicated resurrection from death.

Today, the ankh is still used by the Coptic Church in Egypt for their cross symbol called the *crux ansata*.

See also: Coptic Church.

Aringarosa, Manuel

One of the main characters in *The Da Vinci Code*, Aringarosa is the Opus Dei cardinal who is determined to stop the real identity of the Grail becoming known. Many at first glance see in the name a reference to the seventeenth-century poem about the Black Death in England—"Ring'a Ring'a Rosies." In fact the name is two Italian words: "aringa," meaning "herring," and "rosa," meaning "rose/red"—therefore "red herring." Although he seems to be a powerful figure as he travels through the story, we discover that he has been deceived into thinking that finding the Grail will help Opus Dei. He is horrified to learn of the murders committed during the course of the quest.

See also: Opus Dei.

Asmodeus

Represents the demon who legend says assisted Solomon with the construction of his temple. Asmodeus is believed to be depicted inside the door of the Church of Mary Magdalene in Rennes-le-Château and referenced as the "demon guardian" in the Priory of Sion documents, the Dossiers Secrets. The demon was also venerated by the Cathars as "King of the World." Although not directly referred to in *The Da Vinci Code*, Asmodeus is the shadowy figure that crops up time and again in the stories and legends that Sophie explores in the novel.

See also: Cathars; Dossiers Secrets; Priory of Sion.

Atbash Cipher

Knowledge of this Hebrew coding system is necessary to Sophie Neveu, Robert Langdon, and Leigh Teabing in the novel when they encounter it in a verse that states "and atbash will reveal the truth to thee."

The cipher, which dates from about 500 BC, uses the letters of the Hebrew alphabet in a substitution system where each letter is replaced by one an equal distance from the opposite end of the alphabet. In other words, the first letter is replaced by the last, the second letter by the penultimate one, and so on.

See also: Baphomet; Langdon, Robert; Neveu, Sophie; Teabing, Leigh.

Baphomet

Idol said to have been worshipped by the Knights Templar, a charge that was partly responsible for the order's downfall.

Baphomet is referenced in *The Da Vinci Code* when it forms part of the clue to decoding the cryptex and has to be used in conjunction with the Atbash Cipher in order to reveal the answer.

The word "Baphomet" is, according to some, a corruption of the name Mahomet, as in the Muslim prophet, more commonly known as Muhammad. Or it could be two Greek words joined together that mean "absorption into wisdom." Whatever the etymological derivation of the name, it was claimed that the Knights Templar worshipped in front of a large idol of this Baphomet figure. In modern occult lore, Baphomet is said to have the head of a goat and the body of a man, but with cloven hooves. This description, though, seems to be a fairly modern one and is linked to black magic and satanic rituals, something that was foisted retrospectively onto the Knights Templar in the nineteenth century.

The use of the Atbash Cipher on the word "Baphomet" is accurately portrayed in the novel to reveal the word "Sophia," though written in Hebrew. The reference is important, as Sophie Neveu is the heroine of *The Da Vinci Code*. This hidden meaning was first brought to light by the Dead Sea Scrolls expert, Dr Hugh Schonfeld, author of *The Passover Plot*. Schonfeld has used the Atbash Cipher on many difficult-to-understand passages in the Dead Sea Scrolls to great effect. He decided to apply the cipher to the word "Baphomet" when he became convinced that the Templars must have known about the cipher through their dealings in the Holy Land. The word that is revealed—Sophia—translates as "wisdom." There is, however, one further twist to this tale. The word "Sophia" can also be used in connection with the Mother Goddess, or Sacred Feminine, thereby revealing the tantilising idea that the Templars were actually worshipping the Goddess in secret and in code.

See also: Atbash Cipher; Knights Templar.

Bernard of Clairvaux, St

St Bernard of Clairvaux (1091—1153) was probably the greatest champion of the Knights Templar either within or outside the Church, and his story is important to an understanding of the movement, mentioned throughout *The Da Vinci Code* in the light of its association with the Holy Grail.

St Bernard was one of the foremost spiritual and political figures of the medieval period. He was born in 1091 at the Black Madonna cult center of Les Fontaines in Burgundy, France. His family was minor French nobility; his father was a knight and vassal of the Duke of Burgundy. Bernard was well educated and exhibited a meditative and studious nature from a young age.

In 1113, at the age of 22, Bernard joined the small Cistercian monastery of Citeaux, where he could enjoy the rigors of a religious life. So passionate and eloquent was he in extolling the virtues of such a life that he was soon followed into the monastery by four of his brothers, his widowed father, and thirty of his relatives. At the time, it was stated that his preaching was so persuasive and fervent that "mothers hid their sons, wives their husbands, companions their friends" in case they, too, felt compelled to join him at the monastery.

The Citeaux monastery was very poor, and life within was austere—qualities that appealed to Bernard, who strove to live a life of simplicity and religious meditation. He showed great humility in the way he lived, only eating and sleeping enough to keep himself from fainting. However, word of his self-denial and piety soon spread, and in 1115 he was sent out at the head of a company of other monks to found a new monastery, settling at Clairvaux, Champagne. Within a few years, the Clairvaux monastery proved so successful that it had established 163 other monasteries.

It was at Clairvaux that Bernard began his spiritual writings, and while still a young abbot he published a series of sermons on the Annunciation. In these, he expounded the virtues of the Virgin Mary, especially as a peacemaker. His many sermons highlight his devotion to her, borne out farther by his assertion that as a child he had received divine inspiration by taking three drops of milk from the breast of the Black Madonna statue at Châtillon, an experience that expains his fondness for the Black Madonna cult. St Bernard wrote nearly 90 sermons on the Old Testament's Song of Songs in which he connects the Bride, who calls herself "black, but comely," with Mary of Bethany, another name used at that time for Mary Magdalene.

St Bernard has also been linked with the Knights Templar and was the main champion of the movement to officially recognize them as a military and religious order. His links with the Templars went even deeper than this, however, as St Bernard was instrumental in devising the oath that all Knights Templar had to take. It was called the Templar's Rule, and in it he extolled the Templars to "the obedience of Bethany, the castle of Mary and Martha."

Thanks to his reputation and copious writings, St Bernard's influence and authority gradually extended beyond the confines of Clairvaux, and in 1130 his mediation was sought in an attempt to end the Papal schism that was threatening the stability and coherence of the Church at that time. At the death of Pope Honorius II, rival Popes were elected—Anacletus II and Innocent II. It fell to Bernard to assess each claimant's worth and to decide on the best candidate. After consideration, he settled in favor of Innocent II, who had taken refuge in France. With his usual zeal, St Bernard persuaded France, England, Spain, and Germany to accept Innocent II as their Pope. Eventually, the emperor was also persuaded, and Anacletus II was driven out of Rome.

St Bernard is also remembered for his admonition and ruin of Peter of Abelard, an influential intellectual whose preaching was often considered heretical. St Bernard's tenacious and unrelenting condemnation of Abelard persisted even after the abbot Peter the Venerable had managed to go some way toward healing the rift between the two men. However, it had left Abelard a broken man. St Bernard detested all forms of heresy and fought long and hard against heretics and, in particular, the Cathars.

On behalf of Pope Eugene II, St Bernard preached in favor of a Second Crusade, convincing many to take up arms against the infidel. However, the Second Crusade was a terrible failure. The blame for this fell upon St Bernard, considered the instigator of the war.

In all that he did, St Bernard threw himself into the fold wholeheartedly and enthusiastically. This has given him a reputation for being abusive, insidious, bellicose, belligerent, underhanded, and—oddly, considering his devotion to the Virgin Mary—a misogynist. He died on August 20, 1153, at Clairvaux and was canonized by Pope Alexander III on January 18, 1174.

In his lifetime he founded 163 monasteries throughout Europe, wrote 10 spiritual treatises, over 300 sermons, and 500 extant letters. He is the patron saint of bees, beekeepers, candle makers, chandlers, Gibraltar, and wax refiners and melters.

Unusually for such a strident man of God, St Bernard described Him in very secular terms as "length, width, height, and depth." Here he seems to be alluding to the idea that God in the divine harmony of numbers, for example in the mysterious qualities of the Golden Ratio.

See also: Albigensian Crusade; Black Madonnas; Cathars; Golden ratio; Knights Templar; Mary Magdalene.

Bieil, Sister Sandrine

The name of the guardian nun who let Silas into St-Sulpice church in the middle of the night, is derived from two real-life characters in the Priory of Sion story. Her first name, Sandrine, comes from Gino Sandri, who was Pierre Plantard's personal secretary, Plantard being a Grand Master of the Priory of Sion. Bieil is a reference to the Abbé Bieil, who was the Director General of the Seminary of St-Sulpice in the nineteenth century. Bérenger Saunière, the local parish priest of Rennes-le-Château, was said to have visited Abbé Bieil after he allegedly found secret coded parchments during the renovations of his parish church in 1861.

See also: Plantard, Pierre; Saunière, Jacques; St-Sulpice.

Black Madonnas

Black Madonnas are religious statues of the Madonna and Child, although, as the name suggests, the Madonna is depicted as black skinned. While Dan Brown does not directly refer to them in *The Da Vinci Code*, they are intimately linked with many themes that occur throughout the book, such as goddess worship, Mary Magadelene and the Knights Templar. The statues are found throughout Europe, with the vast majority located in France, where there are over 300. Spain has over 50 Black Madonnas, and there are 19 in Germany and 30 in Italy. Famous Black Madonna statues/shrines are found in Loreto, Zaragoza, Rocamadour, Montserrat, Guadalupe, "Our Lady under the Earth" at Chartres Cathedral, and "Our Lady of Czestochowa" in Poland.

The Black Madonna cult flourished in medieval Europe, when many of the images were made. They mainly take the form of statues carved from either black wood, such as ebony, or wood that is painted black. Other images are carved in stone, and one has been cast in lead. Paintings, frescoes, and icons were also used to depict the Black Madonnas.

The image of the Black Madonna was believed to be a very powerful miracle worker, especially in the areas of fertility and healing. The images were said to hold great knowledge and to have been closely associated with magic. Wherever a Black Madonna was located, a cult sprang up around it, and even today Black Madonna shrines are the focal point of adoration and pilgrimage by large numbers of believers. Despite this, the Church has traditionally not been too happy to welcome the Black Madonnas and their resulting worship.

There are many theories as to why the Madonna and Child should be depicted as black when the Virgin Mary's traditional skin color is white. One theory concludes that the blackness is the result of hundreds of years of candle smoke. However, this fails to take into account that most statues were either carved from ebony or were deliberately painted black. Another theory states that the statues were brought back by the Crusaders from areas inhabited by black people, but studies have shown that the statues were locally made and were not copies of African or Middle Eastern art.

A more logical reason for their blackness is that these images are connected with ancient goddesses, especially as most Black Madonna shrines are located at ancient pagan sites, suggesting a continuation in goddess worship, albeit in another form. The Egyptian goddess Isis, the Roman goddess Diane, and the Asiatic deity Cybele have all at some time been shown as black. Isis has perhaps the most interesting parallels with the Virgin Mary; for example she is traditionally depicted in ancient Egyptian statues with her son, Horus, sitting on her lap. The cult of Isis, who was closely associated with medicine and fertility, spread throughout the Mediterranean region and continued into the Christian era. Even when Christian tradition overtook the older pagan beliefs, much of the iconography and trappings associated with Isis were placed on the Virgin Mary. Hence, both are called the Star of the Sea and Queen of Heaven, both are depicted standing on a crescent moon, or with stars surrounding their head, or as a mother and child. Indeed, the Black Madonna of Notre-Dame du Puy was originally a statue of Isis.

Isis is also linked with Mary Magdalene, whose veneration has flourished alongside the Black Madonna cults. There are 50 Mary Magdalene cult centers around the Mediterranean that also include shrines to the Black Madonna, such as at Marseilles, where one of its three Black Madonna sites is placed outside the underground chapel dedicated to Mary Magdalene. There is a range of hills in France called the

Monts de la Madeleine, and it is around these hills that the greatest density of Black Madonna sites can be found. In a folk tradition directly linking a Black Madonna with Mary Magdalene, the Black Madonna statue, the Madone des Fenêtres (the Madonna of the Windows), was brought to southern France by Mary Magdalene herself.

Many of the Black Madonnas conceal a secret or hidden aspect, such as an association with being underground. In Chartres Cathedral, the Black Madonna statue is called "Our Lady under the Earth," while as we have seen, the Black Madonna statue at Marseilles is located outside an underground chapel. Some researchers suggest that this association indicates the feminine attributes of the divine, with the underground aspect seen as representing the womb of the goddess.

Black Madonnas were venerated by the Knights Templar.

See also: Isis; Knights Templar; Mary Magdalene.

Cathars

In *The Da Vinci Code*, much mention is made of the fact that the Christian Church has in the past put down and violently crushed so-called heretical sects and movements. The Cathars are one such sect, and they play a central and important role in the theories contained within *Holy Blood, Holy Grail*, the book that was used as a basis for the story within *The Da Vinci Code*. The story of the Cathars and their brutal suppression is one of the most important foundation stories of the central mystery that underpins *The Da Vinci*

Code, as it was the Cathars' belief that Jesus and Mary Magdalene were married that contributed to their downfall.

The Cathars were a Christian sect, also known as Albigensians, which was popular in the twelfth and thirteenth centuries in the Languedoc region of France and in northern Italy. They were an offshoot of a heretical sect called the Bogomils of the Balkans, which had existed since the middle of the tenth century. In 1179, at the Third Lateran Council, the Pope publicly denounced the Cathar Church.

The name "Cathar" is thought to come either from the Greek word *katharó*, meaning "pure/purified," or from the German word *ketter* meaning "heretic." Although viewed as heretics by the Catholic Church, Cathars considered themselves to be true Christians, referring to themselves as Christians or Good Men.

The main stronghold for the Cathars was in the Languedoc, today a part of France but at that time a wealthy and independent state. Most of the Languedocian nobility were either Cathars or supportive sympathizers of the Cathar faith. As pacifists, they were no threat to the lords of the land, and their aim of leading a simple, pure, and peaceful life drew many to the Cathar faith.

Eventually, the Cathars fell foul of the Catholic Church because they refused to acknowledge the authority of the Pope: they believed the cross to be an evil symbol of torture and death, and they disliked the trade in holy relics, a trade that was very lucrative to the Church at that time. The Church even sent missionaries—including St Bernard of Clairvaux (see entry)—into Languedoc to win the Cathars over to the true Church, but to no avail.

Due to the obliteration of most of their written records, information on Cathar history, development, and beliefs is sparse, and what does remain comes on the whole from the reports and depositions produced by, and given to, the

Inquisition—not a totally unbiased account by any means. Nevertheless, we know that the central tenet of the Cathar religion was dualism: in other words, they believed in the existence of two opposite and coequal principles of God and the Devil, good and evil, light and darkness. The spiritual realm of heaven was pure and virtuous, whereas the physical, material world was corrupt and evil. Therefore, the immutable, pure soul that belonged to God was trapped within a corrupt and evil body that belonged to the Devil. The pure soul could only be released through the detachment from the material world in order to restore the soul with God. This could be achieved by living a life of absolute purity and abstaining from the evils of the flesh and the physical world.

For the Cathars it followed that if flesh was evil and the product of the Devil, then Christ could not have been born from the Virgin Mary, who although immaculate was still a real woman. The Virgin Birth was therefore nothing more than a symbolic invention, as Christ was a pure, nonphysical spirit who "shadowed in" the Virgin Mary. The Cathars also denied the Crucifixion and Resurrection of Christ, because without a physical body none of this could have happened. The transubstantiation of the bread and wine received at the Eucharist into the body and blood of Christ was also denied by the Cathars, as was the existence of Purgatory and the effectiveness of praying and venerating images. They denied the existence of the Holy Trinity (God the Father, Son, and Holy Spirit), thought that John the Baptist was an instrument of the Devil who had been sent to earth to usurp Christ's mission of salvation, and that Mary Magdalene was the wife of Christ—Christ being a pure spirit but inhabiting a corrupt body, thus being able to marry.

The Cathars rejected the Catholic sacraments (baptism, communion, confirmation, holy orders, penance, supreme unction, and matrimony), receiving instead the *consolamentum* or consolation that transformed the soul back to its perfect state. All those who received the *consolamentum* were called *perfecti*, the pure elite, and from that moment on had to remain pure, abstaining from the corruption of the flesh by eating no meat, poultry, or eggs, not marrying, and becoming celibate. The rigors of life as *perfecti* were such that ordinary believers, *credentes*, did not have to live by these rules, did not have to maintain a strict diet, and could marry and have children. The *perfecti* were dedicated to achieving purity, living an austere, monastic life, and traveling in pairs from place to place, preaching and healing. Just before death, a *credente* received the *consolamentum* and from this moment they entered the state of *endure*, whereby nothing could touch their lips apart from water. As they were now in the state of grace, no woman was allowed to touch them. Women were seen as particularly tainted because of their supposed part in the Fall, whereby the Devil lured souls away from heaven by tempting them with a beautiful woman. Even so, women could and did become *perfecti* and were seen as equals. However, no *perfecti* could touch a pregnant woman due to the corruption of intercourse and because the fetus was considered the Devil's creation.

For those who died without the benefit of the *consolamentum*, their soul would have to be reincarnated again and again, into an animal or human, until it found the body of a Good Man and was able to reach perfection. Martyrdom was a way to avoid having to be reincarnated again, which along with their intent to forgive those who persecuted them may go some way toward explaining why so many thousands of people were prepared to sacrifice their lives for their beliefs. Instead of the Last Judgment of souls—a concept that the Cathars did not accept—they believed that the physical world would cease when all souls had been released from it.

As well as dualism, the Cathars believed in personal salvation, and even ordinary people were encouraged to read the Bible, especially John's Gospel in the New Testament, as the views expressed within John's Gospel were influential in the formation of Cathar beliefs. The only Cathar holy text that we are aware of is the Book of John, which is the same as John's Gospel but with the addition of dualist revelations. The Cathar Church was organized into dioceses with bishops, deacons, and *perfecti*. Services were informal and held in the open, in caves, or in houses.

In 1209, Pope Innocent III called for a Crusade against the Cathars. The Crusade, known as the Albigensian Crusade after the Cathar town of Albi, was particularly bloody and cruel, claiming thousands of lives, Cathar and Christian alike. At this time the Cathars began to fortify many castle fortresses, such as Montségur in southern France, which had originally been used as a site for meditation. However, with the Crusade, Montségur now became a place of refuge. In 1243, Montségur was besieged, but the difficult, mountainous terrain made it hard going for the Crusaders. The Cathars finally surrendered on March 2, 1244, after a ten-month siege, during which time many soldiers are reported to have converted to and joined the ranks of the Cathars. In the terms of surrender, the Cathars were allowed 15 days to prepare themselves for their fate. The night before they were due to give themselves up, four Cathars escaped down the steepest side of the mountain, taking with them the Cathar treasure. Just what this treasure was has never been revealed, and it has been the subject of debate in countless books. It has been conjectured that the treasure may have been the Holy Grail, the fabled "talking head" of the Templars, also known as Baphomet (see entry), important Cathar ritual objects, sacred writings, or, as Lynn Picknett and Clive Prince suggest in *The Templar Revelation*, the treasure may have been the four Cathars themselves. On the day of surrender, all 205 Cathars within Montségur were led singing down the hillside, where they were burned at the stake in the fields below.

The Albigensian Crusade continued for another 11 years until 1255. From then on, it was left to the Inquisition to rid the area of Catharism, which still existed in small pockets in the Pyrenees. Information about this time comes mainly from the small village of Montaillou, from the depositions of those villagers questioned by the Inquisition. By 1320, most Cathar leaders had been burned as heretics, and Catharism was never able to recover.

See also: Albigensian Crusade; Baphomet; Bernard of Clairvaux, St; Holy Blood, Holy Grail.

Chartres Cathedral

The purpose of Robert Langdon's visit to Paris is a lecture about the pagan symbolism that is encoded in the design of Chartres Cathedral.

Chartres Cathedral is situated in the *département* Eure-et-Loir, southwest of Paris, France. Chartres has been an important Christian site since the sixth century AD. By the ninth century it had become a center for the cult of the Madonna, and so it is not surprising that the cathedral is dedicated to St Mary, the Mother of Christ.

In the eleventh century the church that stood at Chartres was replaced by a traditional Romanesque cathedral, which was almost destroyed by fire in the early part of the twelfth century. Thus in 1145 work began on a much grander and impressive cathedral, which over the decades culminated in the magnificent Gothic building that can be seen today. Another fire in 1194 led to a new phase of reconstruction until the cathedral was finally completed in 1225.

Chartres Cathedral was the forerunner of many Gothic cathedrals built in France during this time, with its typical towers, spires, ribbed vaulting, pointed arches, flying buttresses that take the weight of the roof, and the impressive use of stained-glass windows. For the first time, Gothic architecture created a light-filled, awe-inspiring use of space that allowed its designers to incorporate the sacred geometry and symbolism prevalent at this time and known only to an elite few.

The new Gothic architecture appears to coincide with the period following the Second Crusade, in the mid-twelfth century, and for this reason has been seen by some as evidence of returning Crusaders bringing back new ideas and concepts in architecture and thought from exotic parts. Others see this as the result of the secret geometric and architectural methods discovered by the Knights Templar at Jerusalem. Whatever the source of Gothic architecture, its outward magnificence was amplified by the religious and temporal iconography and symbolism as seen in its many statues, carvings, paintings, and scenes. Beyond the more obvious meaning of the decorations and architecture, the designs and depictions conceal other hidden significance and knowledge. Dedicated to the Virgin Mary, the cathedral stresses the feminine principle. The arched entrances and rose window have been likened to the female anatomy, welcoming the observer within. Inside, there is an abundance of female statues and depictions, although a statue of the Queen of Sheba bizarrely has a beard. The oldest depiction of Mary Magdalene can be found on the stained-glass windows. This shows her life in France following the tradition that she went there after the Crucifixion of Christ. In 1200, a labyrinth with an eleven-circuit design of four quadrants was laid into the floor. At its center is a rose design emphasizing enlightenment and the feminine. The floor labyrinth, which pilgrims walked around in meditative prayer, is yet another symbol of feminine anatomy often used at that time.

The cathedral also contains *gematria*, an ancient Hebrew coded cipher that is used to spell out religious phrases. In *gematria*, a numerical value is assigned to each letter, so that words can be equated to a design, and phrases of equivalent value can be said to share a meaning. These can be found encoded throughout the building, as can references to the Ark of the Covenant.

See also: Goddess Worship; Mary Magdalene

Cilice Belt

The belt worn around the thigh by Silas, the albino monk, in the book. A cilice belt is a spiked chain that is worn around the upper thigh for some two hours a day by members of Opus Dei known as Numeraries. Few members will admit to wearing the cilice as it is perhaps the most severe and shocking of the corporal mortifications that they endure. The cilice can leave small prick holes in the flesh when worn, but would have to be extremely tight to inflict the kind of wounds Silas is meant to suffer.

See also: Opus Dei.

Clement V, Pope

The name of Pope Clement V appears in *The Da Vinci Code* in connection with the catastrophe that befell the Knights Templar in 1307. This military order had lost credibility once the Crusader kingdom of Outremer, in the Holy Land, was in the hands of those seen as infidels by the Catholic Church. In discussions with Robert Langdon and Leigh Teabing, Sophie Neveu learns how the Pope condemned practices of the Knights Templar that allegedly included worshiping the head of Baphomet, seen as an idol.

Crowned as Pope Clement V, Bertrand de Gouth was born in 1264 in Gascony, France. He became Archbishop of Bordeaux, France, when he was a chaplain to Pope Boniface VIII, who was in conflict with Philip IV, King of France. The king had taken exception to Boniface's Papal Bull, *Unam Sanctam*, which decreed that Papal authority was supreme. One of Philip's agents held Boniface captive for three days, which was thought to have hastened his death. It is, therefore, not surprising that after his own elevation to the Papacy in 1305, at a coronation attended by King Philip IV, Clement V adopted a cooperative policy toward the French sovereign.

He essentially withdrew *Unam Sanctam*, which had been so offensive to Philip, and also agreed to a trial that brought charges of heresy against his predecessor, Boniface. Clement did find the courage to express his personal opinion that Boniface was innocent of the charges and dragged the trial on for two years, which was long enough for Philip to abandon the process.

Philip IV also targeted the Knights Templar, who through their financial activities were extremely wealthy as an organization. The Knights were accused of heresy, immorality, and greed, and Pope Clement lent his support to repression of the order. This culminated on Friday, October 13, 1307, in the arrest of all the Templars in

France, including the Grand Master, Jacques de Molay.

Torture was used to extract confessions of heresy, and in 1312 Clement suppressed the Order of Knights Templar with a Papal Bull called *Vox in Excelso*. The property of the order was granted to another military sect, the Knights Hospitallers, although in France the king managed to hold onto the estates until his death. Jacques de Molay originally confessed to heresy under torture, but later recanted, and was burned to death in 1314. It was said that as he was dying de Molay prophesied that he would meet both Philip IV and Clement V in death within the year, which proved to be true.

The seat of Papal power, which had always previously been Rome, was relocated to Avignon in France in 1309, and this period, known as the Avignon Papacy, lasted almost 70 years. The political situation in Italy, where rival factions were clashing, deteriorated during Clement's reign, and Papal armies clashed with the city of Venice.

When he died in April 1314, Clement V left as a legacy the reputation as a weak, dutiful Pope who had been manipulated by Philip IV.

See also: Baphomet; Knights Templar.

Codex Leicester

A notebook composed by Leonardo Da Vinci in Milan between 1506 and 1510. The writing is in sepia ink on 18 double-sided sheets of loose-leaf linen paper, with each one folded to make a total of 72 pages. Leonardo addresses "the reader" in several parts of the text.

The Codex Leicester is remarkable for its brilliant scientific notes and deductions as well as for the use of mirror writing employed by Leonardo, which is mimicked in *The Da Vinci Code* by the method that Jacques Saunière uses to disguise the verse to solve cryptex number one. Copious sketches accompany the text, and a wide range of observations is covered, from theories on astronomy to the properties of rocks, water, fossils, air, and celestial light.

The Codex Leicester, named for the English family who bought it in 1717, is now owned by Bill Gates, co-founder of Microsoft and the world's richest man. It is currently on display at the Seattle Art Museum.

See also: Leonardo Da Vinci.

Collet, Jérôme

This lieutenant of police is the assistant to Bezu Fache and seems to follow the action around France as *The Da Vinci Code* gathers pace. "Collet" in French refers to a collar or noose, and in the vernacular the word is used to describe being caught by the police.

See also: Bezu Fache.

Constantine the Great

In *The Da Vinci Code*, Langdon and Teabing need to pass on information to Sophie to help her understand her grandfather's beliefs and actions. They explain that many doctrinal beliefs of the modern Church, and the exclusion of some Gospels from the Bible, were instigated by Constantine the Great.

Constantine was the first "Christian" emperor, although he still held many pagan ideals, and was responsible for uniting the Roman Empire after years of discord. In AD 325 he organized the first council of the Christian Church at Nicaea, which unified the Church and led to the formulation of the concept of the Holy Trinity, one of the most important doctrines of the Christian faith.

Constantine was born in 274 in modern-day Albania. As a soldier in the Roman army, he fought in Diocletian's expedition to Egypt in 296 and in the Persian war. At this time there were two Roman emperors, one situated in the east of the empire, and the other in the west. In 305 the emperors Diocletian and Maximian abdicated and were succeeded by Galerius, emperor in the east, and Constantine's father, Constantinus Chlorus, who ruled in the west. However, after only a year Constantinus Chlorus died, leaving Constantine, whom he had named as his successor, to rule with the emperor Galerius.

The political problems and turmoil within the Roman Empire at this time led to enormous internal fighting, and by 308 there were six emperors ruling simultaneously: three in the east (Galerius, Licinius, and Maximin) and three in the west (Constantine, Maximian, and his son Maxentius). In 309, however, Maxentius deposed his own father, Maximian, who later committed suicide. This now left Constantine and Maxentius, who battled it out for dominion of the Western Roman Empire. It was in 312, before the battle against

41

Maxentius near Rome, that Constantine received a vision of a flaming cross in the sky with the words "In This Conquer." He won the battle, Maxentius drowned, and afterward, because of the vision, Constantine converted to Christianity.

Constantine was now sole emperor in the west and, with the death of Galerius in 311 and Maximin in 313, Licinius was sole emperor in the east. Despite a degree of unity between the two emperors, including the Edict of Milan (313), which afforded toleration and civil rights to Christians throughout the Roman Empire, in 314 Constantine and Licinius met in battle, with the result that the defeated Licinius ceded Illyricum, Pannonia, and Greece to Constantine. Constantine now concentrated on strengthening his borders, and in 323–324 he again defeated, and this time executed, Licinius. Constantine was now sole Roman Emperor. In order to be in a more central position, Constantine moved his capital to Byzantium, which in 330 he renamed Constantinople.

Constantine proved to be a benevolent ruler, rectifying corruption and allowing other religions to continue unmolested. However, in 325 he felt it necessary to call a Church council at Nicaea for all Christian bishops to attend because of the growing tensions and differences within the Christian Church that were threatening the very stability of the empire Constantine had fought hard to obtain. As indicated by the speech he gave to the council, Constantine's desire for harmony was his main concern, as this would ensure peace and prosperity in the empire. There were two important issues that needed attention, the principal being the Arian heresy and the other being the disparate dates for Easter, both of which were causing division.

The Arian heresy denied the divinity of Jesus Christ, and after much discussion the bishops produced a creed—the Creed of Nicaea—that stated the Christian belief in God the

Father, God the Son, and God the Holy Spirit, thus confirming the divinity of Christ. The date for Easter was set at the Sunday after the first full moon of the vernal equinox (although the date of the vernal equinox remained a point of contention for years to come). Many of the books of what we now know as the New Testament were supposedly chosen at the Council of Nicaea.

Despite Constantine's leanings toward Christianity, he was not baptized until 326. It has been suggested that Constantine chose Christianity as the official religion of the Roman Empire as a way of using the potency of the Christian God to profit the empire. Whatever his reasons, Constantine's patronage of Christianity ensured its growth, power, and affluence, and, although he allowed pagan temples to continue, their wealth was redistributed to Christian churches.

Unfortunately, Constantine's desire for harmony was not reflected in his personal life, and in 326 his son Crispus was executed for treason, as was his second wife Fausta in 327. On May 22, 337, Constantine died. Having achieved control over a united empire, he passed it on to his three sons, Constantius, Constantine, and Constans, thus dividing the Roman Empire once more.

See also: Council of Nicaea.

Coptic Church

The Nag Hammadi texts, found in 1945 in Egypt and sometimes known as the Lost Gospels, are texts written in the Coptic language, an ancient language that is still used to this day by Coptic Christians in Egypt. In *The Da Vinci Code*, mention is made of these so-called Lost Gospels, with the claim being that they were deliberately left out of the New Testament because of their Gnostic content. These texts were undoubtedly a product of the early Coptic Church.

The Coptic Church is the name given to the Christian Church in Egypt. The Coptic Church is based on the teachings of St Mark, who brought Christianity to Egypt early in the first century. Since this time, the Coptic Church has had its own Pope, with the present incumbent, Pope Shenouda III, being the 117th patriarch of Alexandria since St Mark.

The see of Alexandria, considered second only to Rome, has played an integral role in Christian theology. However, in 451, following the Council of Chalcedony, a split occurred between the Copts and the rest of Christianity, resulting in the Coptic Church following their Pope Dioscorus and calling themselves orthodox. Steps were taken to reunite the two Churches, but it was not until the Florence Council in 1443 that a union was signed (although not acted on). In 1582 and 1814, other unions were attempted, but to no avail.

The Coptic Church has suffered greatly from persecution in its past, in particular under the Roman Emperor Diocletian. To remember the faithful who died, the Coptic Church introduced the Calendar of Martyrs on August 29, 284. Under Arab rule, Copts were free to carry out their religious practices, but in order to do so they had to pay a special tax called *gezya*, which was finally abolished in 1855. Although the Coptic Church can be found throughout Egypt, its followers form a very small proportion of the

Egyptian population. However, the Coptic Church is not confined to Egypt alone, having many branches worldwide.

As in the Catholic Church, the Coptic Church has seven sacraments (baptism, communion, confirmation, penance, holy orders, matrimony, and extreme unction). The Coptic Church forbids the worship of saints, although to ask for their help through prayer is encouraged. The most highly regarded saint is the Virgin Mary.

Seven major feasts are observed by the Coptic Church (the Annunciation, Christmas, the Baptism of Christ, Palm Sunday, Easter, the Ascension, and Pentecost) and seven minor feasts (the Circumcision of Christ, the Entrance of Christ into the Temple, the Flight of the Holy Family into Egypt, the Miracle at Cana, the Transfiguration of Christ, Maundy Thursday, and Thomas's Sunday). In addition, there are also monthly feasts, weekly feasts, and the feasts of saints, which usually commemorate their martyrdom. As well as Feast Days, fasting is an integral part of the Coptic Church, with 210 days of the year set aside for this practice. On these days it is forbidden to eat any animal produce and nothing whatsoever between sunrise and sunset.

The Coptic Church has a Pope at its head, and below the Pope there are over 60 bishops. The Pope and bishops have to be monks. The Coptic Pope is not considered infallible, and issues concerning faith and other matters are discussed at the Coptic Orthodox Holy Synod by the Pope and his bishops. Coptic priests are responsible for congregational matters and, unlike within the Catholic Church, priests are expected to marry.

The Coptic monasteries of St Anthony, St Catherine, and St Samuel are the oldest religious establishments in Christendom.

See also: Constantine the Great; Council of Nicaea.

Council of Nicaea

This council ruled on many aspects that *The Da Vinci Code* explores throughout the novel. Teabing claims in the book that it was the Council of Nicaea that decided which gospels would be included in the New Testament and which should be left out. Although we do not know this is historically accurate, the council did rule on one key issue that is at the heart of the mystery that the characters seek to solve—whether or not Jesus was mortal (and therefore able to marry and bear children). The belief that Christ was mortal was known as the Arian heresy. The Council of Nicaea, however, decreed that Christ was divine and therefore could not possibly have been married.

Emperor Constantine called the first ecumenical council of the Church in 325, primarily to end the division and disharmony within the Church caused by the Arian heresy. Its other aim was to establish a common date for Easter. In discussing and settling the issue of the Arian heresy, the Council of Nicaea formulated one of the most important doctrines of the Christian faith: namely, the Holy Trinity of God the Father, God the Son, and God the Holy Spirit.

The importance of settling these issues is shown by Constantine's intention for all bishops to attend. To ensure their arrival, the bishops were given free use of the imperial transportation system, enabling them to travel without cost to themselves and under the protection of the Roman army. Originally, a council was to convene in Ancyra, but Constantine changed the location to Nicaea (known today as Iznik, in Turkey), further west, thus making it easier for the bishops from Italy and Europe to attend, and so that he himself could watch the proceedings and participate in them.

The council convened on June 19, 325, and sat for two months, with various reports stating that between 250 and 320 bishops were present. Emperor Constantine arrived early in July and made a speech to the council on the importance of harmony. There are three documents which survive from the council: the Creed of Nicaea, the canons, and a letter to the Egyptian Church.

The Arian heresy had permeated all levels of Christianity throughout the Roman Empire. Constantine wanted an undivided, harmonious Church in order to promote peace and prosperity, and was concerned that the internal dissension caused by Arianism would threaten the stability of the empire. Arianism was born out of the unorthodox opinions of Arius, a Christian from Alexandria in Egypt. He held the view that Christ was not a deity but the "first and greatest of God's creatures." The lack of Christ's divinity meant that He was subject to sin and alteration. Arius asserted that Christ had a beginning, unlike God who "is without beginning" and that "before his generation he was not."

It is believed that Constantine himself was influenced by the Arianist view as well as by some Arian bishops. It therefore shows Constantine's strong desire to end the developing schism that he was prepared to stand behind the decision of the council that condemned Arianism and confirmed the established doctrine of the Church. The bishops produced a creed to emphasize the divinity of Christ and the relationship of God, Christ, and the Holy Spirit. The Creed of Nicaea stated:

We believe in one God the Father all powerful, maker of all things both seen and unseen. And in one Lord Jesus Christ, the Son of God, the only-begotten begotten from the Father, that is from the substance of the Father, God from God, light from light, true God from true God, begotten not made, consubstantial with the Father, through whom all things came to be, both those in heaven and those in earth; for us humans and for our salvation he came down and became incarnate, became human, suffered and rose up on the third day, went up into the heavens, is coming to judge the living and the dead. And in the Holy Spirit.

In this Creed the bishops confirmed that Christ was not created by God the Father but was of the same substance as Him ("that is from the substance of the Father"); that God the Father and Christ were both God ("God from God, light from light, true God from true God"); and that Christ was divine and one with the Father ("consubstantial with the Father"). The term "consubstantial" (Greek *homoousios*) has been the subject of much debate over the years and appears to have been a term decided on by Constantine himself.

A note was added to the Creed to the effect that the Catholic and Apostolic Church denounced anyone agreeing with Arian sentiments. It was signed by all the bishops present apart from Secundus of Ptolemais and Theonas of Marmarica, whom Constantine duly banished, along with Arius. It is to be noted that this was not the final resolution to the question of the Trinity, with further debate on this subject in the years to come. The Creed of Nicaea was rectified further at the First Council of Constantinople in 381, and this is known to us as the Nicene Creed.

The other main issue, that of Easter, was also settled by the council, which decided that Easter should fall on the Sunday after the first full moon of the vernal equinox (although the date of the vernal equinox remained a point of contention for years to come).

The aim of the 20 canons was to establish a universal Church with common observances and practices throughout. Accordingly, the geographical areas of authority and jurisdiction for Rome, Alexandria, Antioch, and Jerusalem were established as well as other, smaller issues. These included not allowing anyone who had purposefully castrated themselves to become priests and not allowing anyone who had been excommunicated to join a church in another diocese. The council also stated that any clergy charging interest on loans were to be dismissed from the priesthood, and debated who can or cannot give or receive communion.

See also: Constantine the Great.

Dossiers Secrets

Both Robert Langdon and Leigh Teabing are described in *The Da Vinci Code* as being well versed in the Dossiers Secrets. When the police search Teabing's house they find copies of documents and photographs, which they collect as evidence without appreciating what they are.

The Dossiers Secrets are generally regarded as the secret archives of the Priory of Sion. Specifically, the Dossiers Secrets constitute a file, dated 1967, of texts allegedly written by a man named Henri Lobineau and compiled by Philippe Toscan du Plantier. It contains newspaper clippings, assorted letters, genealogy charts, and a "tableau," dated 1956, relating the early history of the Priory of Sion and incorporating the Grand Master lists.

The collection was deposited in the Bibliothèque Nationale in France. It had been made public as part of an ongoing release of information which has been leaked anonymously by someone within the Priory of Sion since 1956. At first, the Dossiers identified Henri Lobineau as the pseudonym of one Leo Schidlof, whose inspiration for the name had presumably come from Rue Lobineau, a real street near the church of St-Sulpice. However, after the authors of *Holy Blood, Holy Grail* contacted the late Schidlof's daughter, who denied her father's involvement in any secret society, another secret communiqué was issued which stated that Henri Lobineau was actually the pseudonym of a French aristocrat by the name of Henri de Lénoncourt.

Although the contents of the Dossiers Secrets are sprinkled with a multitude of tantalizing clues about the Priory of Sion, by far the most intriguing item is the page entitled Planche Number 4, which summarizes the history and structure of the order. In addition to the Grand Master list (see separate entry), it is revealed that there were 27 commandaries and one "arch," called "Beth-Ania," which presumably oversaw the commandaries. The arch was located in Rennes-le-Château, in the Aude region of southern France, and the most important commandaries were to be found in Bourges, Gisors, Jarnac, Mont-St-Michel, Montrevel, and Paris.

Furthermore, according to the Dossiers Secrets, the Priory of Sion was said to comprise 1,093 members, structured around seven grades with membership numbers in each grade determined by multiples of three:

1. Preux (729 members)
2. Ecuyers (243 members)
3. Chevaliers (81 members)
4. Commandeurs (27 members)
5. Croisés de St-John (9 members)
6. Princes Noachites de Notre-Dame (3 members)
7. Nautonnier (1 Grandmaster)

In *The Da Vinci Code*, it was the top four members in the sixth and seventh grades, the three Princes and the Nautonnier, who were murdered.

The genealogies contained within the Dossiers Secrets

detail the lineages of what have come to be regarded as the "bloodline" families—in other words, the families who, it is claimed, are descendants of the supposed union between Jesus and Mary Magdalene. These include the St-Clairs, the Blancheforts, the Merovingians, and the House of Plantard. They also contain the genealogies of the Kings of Jerusalem and of Godfroy de Bouillon, who founded the original Order of Sion in 1090 in the Holy Land.

See also: Grand Masters of Priory of Sion; Merovingians; Plantard, Pierre; Priory of Sion.

Fache, Bezu

The name of a character in *The Da Vinci Code* who, as a captain in the French police, is responsible for investigating the death of Jacques Saunière, the curator at the Louvre museum. His surname, "fache," means "cross" or "angry" in French, which is consistent with his curt and abrasive manner. When Robert Langdon meets Fache, he notices that the policeman is wearing a *crux gemmata*, a crucifix or cross representing Christ and His disciples.

His first name, Bezu, is a location in southern France with close associations to two organizations repeatedly discussed in the book. The Knights Templar had a fortress on the mountain at Bezu, where they were believed to be guarding a treasure. The peak at Bezu is southeast of Rennes-le-Château, the village where Bérenger Saunière, a priest, arrived in 1885. The activities of this priest, and the mystery surrounding them, are discussed in the book *Holy Blood, Holy Grail*.

Teabing describes the book as "the best-known tome" on the bloodline of Christ, when he and Langdon are telling Sophie about the mystery of the Holy Grail.

See also: Holy Blood, Holy Grail; Knights Templar; Priory of Sion.

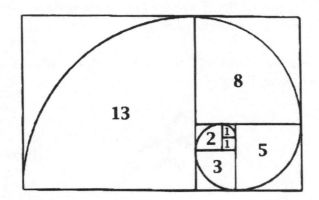

Fibonacci Sequence

At the site where Jacques Saunière's body is found at the start of the book, some numbers are written on the floor. Sophie, his granddaughter, recognizes the sequence and interprets it as a sign from him, although it takes time for the full significance to emerge. Once she has the key to the bank safe-deposit box and realizes that she needs an account number to access the box, the numbers are arranged in ascending order to provide the solution.

Created by Leonardo Fibonacci, the Fibonacci sequence is an infinite sequence of numbers, beginning: 1, 1, 2, 3, 5, 8, 13... where each number is the sum of the two numbers preceding it. Thus: $1 + 1 = 2$, $1 + 2 = 3$, $2 + 3 = 5$, $3 + 5 = 8$, $5 + 8 = 13$, and so on. For any value larger than 3 in the sequence, the ratio between any two consecutive numbers is 1:1.618, or the Golden Ratio.

The Fibonacci sequence can be seen in nature, where the sunflower, for instance, has 21 spirals on its head in one direction and 34 going in the other—consecutive Fibonacci numbers. The outside of a pinecone has spirals that run clockwise and counterclockwise, and the ratio of the number of spirals is sequential Fibonacci values. In the elegant curves of a nautilus shell, each complete new revolution will be a ratio of 1:1.618, when compared to the distance from the center of the previous spiral.

Fibonacci was born in Pisa, Italy, in 1170. He grew up and was educated in Bugia, North Africa, modern-day Bejaia in Algeria, returning to Pisa in around 1200. Fibonacci was undoubtedly influenced and possibly tutored by Arab mathematicians during this formative time. He wrote many mathematical texts and made some significant mathematical discoveries, helping to make his works very popular in Italy and bringing him to the attention of the Holy Roman Emperor at the time, Frederick II, who invited him to his court in Pisa. Fibonacci died in 1250.

See also: Golden Ratio; Golden Rectangle.

Gnomon at St-Sulpice

The gnomon, or sundial, in the Church of St-Sulpice in Paris, or more specifically at the base of the obelisk that forms part of it, is the hiding place of the keystone Silas is looking for. He smashes a floor tile covering a hollow space to discover not the map he is expecting but a biblical quotation from Job.

It was the pastor of St-Sulpice, Jean-Baptiste Languet de

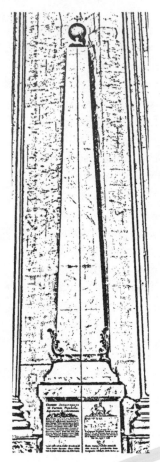

Gergy (1675—1750), who was responsible for raising funds to build the gnomon in 1737. The pastor wanted to establish the exact timing of the equinoxes so that he could calculate the date on which Easter would fall every year. Easter is literally a movable feast, which should be celebrated at the full moon that follows the spring equinox. There are, therefore, sound theological reasons for the construction of this astronomical device within the church.

Sundials have been used to calculate time for many millennia: the ancient Egyptians knew that if a pole is sunk vertically in the ground, the shadow cast by the sun at noon will vary in length over time.

In this case the gnomon consists of a brass line that runs north–south set into the floor of the transept of the church. A white marble obelisk with the brass line continuing up the center has a mark (of the sign Capricorn) where the sun strikes at the winter solstice, December 21. As the seasons pass, the sun, which enters through an opening in a window in the south transept, moves along the line. This opening, which once contained a lens, is 82 feet above floor level. An engraved marble plaque on the pavement of the south transept indicates the position of the sun on June 21, the summer solstice. The equinoxes of March 21 and September 21 have an oval copper plaque nestling behind the altar rail to register their passage.

The obelisk bears an inscription on its base commemorating the purpose of the construction of the sundial. Since the loyal inscription contained the names of the king and ministers, it fell victim to the French Revolution and is now defaced. There are also marked on the obelisk the signs for Aquarius and Sagittarius at the point where the sun strikes on January 21 and November 21.

Another observation could be made from the measurements taken at St-Sulpice. Astronomers from the Paris Observatory, notably Giovanni Cassini, used the measurements to study the rotation of the earth. As the earth rotates in its orbit around the sun, the axis on which it turns pivots slowly over time. From results Cassini obtained, the astronomers calculated that the axis of the earth decreases by 45 seconds of degree every 100 years. This is very close to the accepted value today of 46.85 seconds derived from modern precision instruments.

See also: Bieil, Sister Sandrine; St-Sulpice.

Gnostics

Gnosticism is the term used to refer to a heretical belief system that was prevalent by the second century AD and which the early Christian Church attacked. The term derives from the Greek word *gnosis*, meaning "knowledge," and the concept that they were privy to secret knowledge runs through various Gnostic sects.

Until the twentieth century, most information regarding Gnostic sects or leaders came from the Christian writers who denounced them, which casts doubt on the validity of these sources. When some ancient Gnostic texts were discovered in Egypt in 1945, important first-hand records of these ancient beliefs were seen for the first time. These became known as the Nag Hammadi texts, named for the village near which they were found. The most famous is the Gospel of Thomas. The Nag Hammadi texts were originally written in Greek in the first or second centuries AD and translated into Coptic in the third and fourth centuries.

In *The Da Vinci Code*, the Gnostic Gospels are mentioned in the context of the actions by the Roman Emperor Constantine the Great, who supposedly selected the "approved" versions of the Gospels that eventually became the Bible as we know it. This process was the product of the Council of Nicaea, which met in AD 325 and at which the doctrines of the Catholic Church were fixed. Once the main tenets of the Church had been established, those who held alternative beliefs were condemned as heretics.

The origins of Gnosticism are debated by scholars, who vary in their opinions as to whether its roots are pagan with elements of Platonism or, alternatively, are derived from Judaism. The basic Gnostic belief is that there is a good true God, but that this world and the matter within it were created by a lesser evil God, called the Demiurge. The true God is referred to as the first Aeon, and from this derive 30 pairs of other Aeons in a sequence of lower significance. The combined Aeons make up the concept of the complete God, known as Pleroma. Interestingly, the last pair of Aeons are Christ and Sophia. Sophie Neveu is the character in *The Da Vinci Code* who discovers information as she investigates her grandfather's murder—in other words, she is achieving gnosis.

When Christ is sent to earth as the human Jesus, His purpose is to give mankind gnosis so that they can escape the imperfect physical world and return to the Pleroma. There are then three types of humans: hylics, who are bound to evil matter and cannot be saved; psychics, who can be partly saved as they have a soul; and pneumatics, who can return to the Pleroma if they achieve gnosis.

Two of the most notable Gnostics are Basilides and Valentius, both of whom attracted followers in the second century AD. Basilides, from Alexandria, Egypt, active from 120 to 145, wrote *Exegitica* and claimed to possess a secret tradition handed down from St Peter and St Matthias. Valentius was educated in Alexandria and then taught in Rome from 135; he is believed to have been the author of the Gnostic Gospel of Truth, one of the Nag Hammadi texts.

In addition to the followers of Basilides and Valentius, there have been numerous other Gnostic sects. In the Persian tradition, there was Manichaeism, which is now extinct, and Mandaeanism, which survives in isolated areas of Iran and Iraq. In Europe, the Bogomils were widespread in the area of modern Bulgaria in the tenth to thirteenth centuries, but probably the most famous Gnostic sect was the Cathars, also known as the Albigensians.

See also: Albigensian Crusade, Cathars; Constantine the Great; Council of Nicaea.

Goddess Worship

The Da Vinci Code characters of Jacques Saunière and Robert Langdon have expertise in the goddess and her symbolism. It is made clear in the novel that Saunière had expanded the collection of goddess figures in the Louvre and that Robert

Langdon was preparing a manuscript for a new book, titled *Symbols of the Lost Sacred Feminine*.

Within *The Da Vinci Code*, it is also made clear that the figure of Mary Magdalene represents and symbolizes the original goddess and the subsequent worship of her.

Goddess worship can be traced back to at least 35,000 BC, and as such it can be claimed that goddess worship is the oldest of the world religions, having a history and heritage that stretches back into the mists of time itself. With the emergence of Cro-Magnon man, the first recognizable humans, in around 35,000 BC, we first start to see imagery and artwork that seem to represent the goddess figure. *The Language of the Goddess*, a book by Marija Gimbutas, is a good place to view some of these figures.

Seen originally as the mother of all things, the evolution of the goddess figure can be traced throughout the Middle East and Europe and also India, where the Hindu religion has taken goddess worship to a higher spiritual platform. In biblical times, goddess worship was practiced throughout the Holy Land, with the goddess Asherah being especially venerated and, in some traditions, seen as the consort of Yahweh, or God Himself. Asherah was symbolized at many sites by so-called Asherah Stones, upright standing stones that not only represented the goddess but also seem to have the dual symbolism of the phallus as well. At this time, a concerted effort to suppress the worship or veneration of the goddess was undertaken, with a much more patriarchal society emerging; the god, king, priest, and father replacing the goddess, queen, priestess, and mother. Indeed, it is only in recent years that the Christian Church has elected women priests, showing how complete the subjugation of woman was by the Judeo-Christian doctrine. In Islam, too, it seems that suppression of the female has taken place, with some researchers theorizing that the origins of the supreme Islamic deity Allah lie in the goddess Al-lat, who was associated with the Kaaba at Mecca, a pre-Muslim shrine that was usurped for the Islamic faith by Muhammad himself.

In Egypt, Isis was seen as the ultimate embodiment of the feminine, with a number of other goddesses also making up the litany of higher deities—although, in Egypt, the goddess was seen as the womb that enabled the birth of the god, in this case Horus the Younger, with the name of the goddess Hathor literally meaning "house of Horus."

At the Council of Ephesus in AD 431, a meeting of Christian bishops established that the Virgin Mary should be known as Theotokos, or "Mother of God," so setting her in the role of the goddess, though they were careful not to give her the usual fertility attributes associated with goddess figures. The later worship of the Black Madonnas throughout Europe seems to be a recognition of the figure of the Virgin Mary as a goddess in her own right—though in the Roman Catholic Church Mary is seen as a submissive mother and as a compliant figure, so negating many of the characteristics that are usually associated with the goddess.

In medieval Europe, many thousands of women were burned at the stake for witchcraft. This crusade against the feminine once more suppressed the rise of female independence and power, and subjugated the goddess worship that was gaining momentum.

Goddess cults saw something of a revival in the nineteenth century, with the re-emergence of the Wicca religion in northern Europe. Also known as "white witchcraft," Wicca holds the goddess in high esteem, with an underlying belief in an equilibrium between the god and goddess, a duality of sorts. Many modern feminist movements have also elevated the goddess to newfound heights, and today, once again, goddess veneration is enjoying a renaissance.

The goddess was associated with the moon from ancient

times. This association is bound in with the bodily cycles of the female and the lunar cycles of the moon, and also with the fact that the moon has three phases—waxing, full, and waning—corresponding to the three phases of the goddess: maiden, mother, and crone. Each of these goddess phases had a distinct purpose and value. The maiden represented youth, sexuality, and vigor; the mother represented the embodiment of female power, fertility, and the nurturing impulse; the crone represented experience, compassion, and, above all, wisdom.

Today, the veneration and understanding of goddess energy and spirituality are once more to the fore. In the millennia of modern human beings' existence, the figure of the goddess has been omnipresent. I suspect that as long as mankind will walk the planet, this will be the case. The goddess can truly claim to be the original and oldest deity.

See also: Black Madonnas; Isis; Mary Magdalene.

Golden Ratio

As Sophie Neveu and Robert Langdon are escaping the Louvre, they discuss the meaning of the numbers scrawled beside the body of Saunière. Noting that the numbers from the Fibonacci sequence (see entry), they discuss its relation to the Golden Ratio. This same sequence is then found to be the combination needed at the Zurich Depository Bank. The Golden Ratio is a subject that Langdon has lectured on to students at Harvard, where he works.

Known by the Greek letter phi (φ), the Golden Ratio is an irrational number (i.e. one that cannot be expressed as the

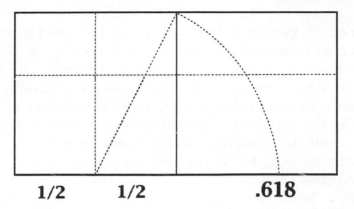

1/2   **1/2**   **.618**

ratio or fraction of two whole numbers) with several curious properties. We can define it as the number that is equal to its own reciprocal plus one: $\phi = {}^{1}/\phi + 1$, with its value commonly expressed as 1.618,033,989. Its digits were calculated to 10 million places in 1996, and they never repeat. It is related to Fibonacci numbers in that if you divide two consecutive numbers in the Fibonacci sequence, the answer is always an approximation of phi.

Also known as the Divine Proportion, the Golden Mean, or the Golden Section, this ratio is found with surprising frequency in natural structures as well as man-made art and architecture, where the ratio of length to width of approximately 1.618 is seen as visually pleasing. The ratio's strange properties meant it was historically seen as divine in its makeup and infinite in its meaning. The ancient Greeks, for example, believed that understanding the ratio would help one to get closer to God: God was "in" the number.

It is certainly true that harmony can be expressed in numbers, whether in pictorial or architectural space, in the realm of music, or indeed in nature. The harmony of the Golden Ratio or Divine Proportion turns up naturally in many places. In the human body, the ventricles of the human heart reset themselves at the Golden Ratio point of the heart's rhythmic cycle. The human face incorporates the ratio in its proportions. If you divide the pitch of a DNA spiral or a mollusc shell by its diameter, you get the Golden Ratio. And if you look at the way leaves grow on the stem of a plant, you can see that each leaf grows at a different angle from the leaf below. The most common angle between successive leaves is directly related to the Golden Ratio.

In art and architecture, too, the famed harmonious properties of the Golden Ratio have been used to great effect. The dimensions of the King's Chamber of the Great Pyramid in Egypt are based upon the Golden Ratio; the architect Le Corbusier designed his Modulor system around the use of the ratio; the painter Mondrian based most of his work on the Golden Ratio; Leonardo included it in many of his paintings and Claude Debussy used its properties in his music. The Golden Ratio also crops up in some very unlikely places: widescreen televisions, postcards, credit cards and photographs all commonly conform to its proportions. And many experiments have been carried out to prove that the proportions of top models' faces conform more closely to the Golden Ratio than the rest of the population, which is supposedly why we find them beautiful.

Lucia Pacioli, a friend of Leonardo Da Vinci whom he met while working at the court of Ludovico Sforza, Duke of Milan, wrote a major treatise on the Golden Section, entitled *Divina Proportione*. In this book, Pacioli attempts to explain the meaning of the Divine Proportion in a logical, scientific manner, though he believed its elusive quality reflected the mystery of God. This and other works of Pacioli seem to have influenced Leonardo a great deal, and the two became firm friends, even working on mathematical problems together. The use of the Golden Ratio is evident within the major works of Leonardo, who for a long time had shown a great interest in the mathematics of art and nature. Like the brilliant Pythagoras before him, Leonardo had made an in-depth study of the human figure, showing how all of its major parts were related to the Golden Ratio. It has been said that Leonardo's great unfinished painting, *St Jerome*, which shows the saint with a lion at his feet, was painted in a deliberate style so as to make sure a Golden Rectangle (see entry) fits around the central figure. With Leonardo's love of "geometrical recreations" this seems a reasonable assumption. The *Mona Lisa*'s face, too, fits inside a perfect Golden Rectangle.

After Leonardo, artists such as Raphael and Michelangelo made great use of the Golden Ratio to construct their works. Michelangelo's breathtaking sculpture *David* conforms to the Golden Ratio, from the location of the navel with respect to the height and placement of the joints in the fingers.

The builders of the medieval and Gothic churches and cathedrals of Europe also erected these amazing structures to conform to the Golden Ratio. In this respect, God really was in the numbers.

See also: *Fibonacci Sequence; Golden Rectangle.*

Golden Rectangle

Several works by Leonardo Da Vinci are important to the plot of *The Da Vinci Code*, either as clues to solve puzzles, i.e. the *Mona Lisa* and *Madonna of the Rocks*, or as examples of ideas that may be encoded in the picture, e.g. *The Last Supper*. Like many Renaissance artists, Leonardo used the Golden Rectangle in these paintings.

The Golden Rectangle is one whose sides are in the proportion of the Golden Ratio: in other words, the longer side is 1.618 times longer than the shorter side. The Golden Ratio and Rectangle are seen as aesthetically pleasing forms and are found in many areas of art and culture the world over. A good example of this would be the Parthenon in Athens, Greece, where the front of the Parthenon can be comfortably framed within a Golden Rectangle.

As an example of how Da Vinci used the Golden Rectangle, his drawing of the *Vitruvian Man* has the outlines of a rectangle based on the head, one on the torso, and another over the legs. The face of the *Mona Lisa* also fits into a Golden Rectangle, and in the composition of *The Last Supper* the same proportions are used.

See also: Fibonacci Sequence; Golden Ratio; Last Supper, The; Madonna of the Rocks; Mona Lisa.

Grand Masters of the Priory of Sion

Jacques Saunière is the curator at the Louvre in Paris, who at the start of *The Da Vinci Code* is murdered but who leaves a trail of clues for his granddaughter, Sophie Neveu, to follow. As she explores the circumstances of his death, helped by Robert Langdon, it emerges that Jacques Saunière was the supposed Grand Master of the Priory of Sion.

The Priory documents, known as the Dossiers Secrets, list the following people as Grand Masters of the Priory of Sion:

Jean de Gisors	(1188—1220)
Marie de St-Clair	(1220—66)
Guillaume de Gisors	(1266—1307)
Édouard de Bar	(1307—36)

(*Above*) The most famous painting in the world, the *Mona Lisa* – but what did her enigmatic smile hide? Could this be a self-portrait of Leonardo himself (*right*)?

Leonardo's *Adoration of the Magi*. Recent research has shown that the original painting underneath had a radically different theme.

The first version
of Leonardo's
*Madonna of the
Rocks* (*left*), now
hanging in the
Louvre, Paris,
was considered
so subversive
that a second
version (*below*)
had to be
painted, now in
the National
Gallery, London.

(*Left*) Leonardo's masterpiece, *The Last Supper*. The close-up (*above*) shows the controversial 'disembodied hand' holding a knife, and the figure to the left of Jesus who some researchers claim is a woman. If so, could this be a representation of Mary Magdalene, who many believe to have been the consort of Jesus?

(*Above*) The famous glass and steel pyramid at the entrance to the Louvre Museum in Paris, France.

(*Right*) St-Sulpice Church, Paris, home of the mysterious Gnomon and Rose Line.

(*Right*) Temple Church in London is an original Knights Templar site of worship. Built in the twelfth century, the church is still used to this day.

(*Left*) The beautiful monument to Newton, housed in Westminster Abbey, London.

(*Above*) Rosslyn Chapel, near Edinburgh, Scotland, is famous for its extraordinary carvings that have yet to be decoded. Contrary to popular belief, it was not built by the Knights Templar.

(*Below*) Seemingly suspended in mid-air, the Pyramide Inversée in the Louvre, Paris, delicately hovers above a small stone pyramid on the floor.

Jeanne de Bar	(1336—51)
Blanche d'Evreux	(1366—98)
Nicolas Flamel	(1398—1418)
René d'Anjou	(1418—80)
Iolande de Bar	(1480—83)
Sandro Filipepi	(1483—1510)
Leonardo Da Vinci	(1510—19)
Connétable de Bourbon	(1519—27)
Ferdinand de Gonzague	(1527—75)
Louis de Nevers	(1575—95)
Robert Fludd	(1595—1637)
J. Valentin Andrea	(1637—54)
Robert Boyle	(1654—91)
Isaac Newton	(1691—1727)
Charles Radclyffe	(1727—46)
Charles de Lorraine	(1746—80)
Maximilian de Lorraine	(1780—1801)
Charles Nodier	(1801—44)
Victor Hugo	(1844—85)
Claude Debussy	(1885—1918)
Jean Cocteau	(1918—63)

See also: *Dossier Secrets*; *Langdon, Robert*; *Neveu, Sophie*;
Newton, Sir Isaac; *Priory of Sion*; *Saunière, Jacques*.

Heretics

The theory that there exists a bloodline of Christ, descended
to modern times, underpins the plot of *The Da Vinci Code*, a
theory that has been postulated in books such as *Holy Blood,
Holy Grail* and *The Templar Revelation*. This theory in itself

can be seen as a modern-day heresy in light of traditional Christian teachings.

As a specific subject in the novel, heretics are described to Sophie as those who choose to follow the original history of Christ as a mortal man rather than as the divine figure outlined at the Council of Nicaea.

Within Christianity, a heretic is one who holds views that contradict the orthodoxy or core values and doctrines of the Church. Heresy is distinguished from apostasy, the complete abandonment of faith, as it is from schism, the splitting of or from the Church, usually brought about by disputes and arguments about hierarchy and discipline and not by matters of doctrine.

Heretics actually consider themselves as Church members, but, in a doctrinal controversy, as true believers. Arianism was one such heresy that threatened the early Church. Arius was a fourth-century priest of Alexandria, who taught that God created a son before all things, who was the first living creature, but who was neither equal to nor co-eternal with the father. In this heresy, according to Arius, Jesus was a supernatural creature—not quite human and not quite divine.

Heresy was usually dealt with by excommunication, especially in the case of individuals and small heretical groups—though in the medieval age the Church also undertook military campaigns. Famously, one such campaign was against the Cathars (1208), the religious sect based in southern France. The Inquisition was a particularly punitive and vicious campaign against heresy in medieval times.

See also: Albigensian Crusade; Cathars; Council of Nicaea; Holy Blood, Holy Grail; Neveu, Sophie.

Hieros Gamos

The sacred sexual ritual that Sophie accidentally witnessed her grandfather, Jacques Saunière, watched by a group of initiates, which led to her breaking contact with him for 10 years.

The term "Hieros Gamos" is derived from the Greek words meaning "sacred marriage." Having its roots in ancient fertility cults, the Hieros Gamos ritual evolved into a highly developed spiritual discipline that enabled a man to attain "gnosis," or direct knowledge of the divine, through ritualized sexual union with a woman trained as a priestess. The theory is based on the philosophy that man is fundamentally incomplete and can reach divinity only by "marrying" the feminine principles in a spiritual and physical manner, which triggers an altered state of consciousness at the moment of climax.

This state is also symbolized by Hermaphrodite, a male/female duality seen as the fusion of the god Hermes and the goddess Aphrodite. Furthermore, it is said by some that cryptic references within medieval texts relating to alchemy (the art of transformation) actually relate to sexual ritual on a higher level. The medieval heretics became adept at developing a symbolic language through which to discuss these matters, with the rose being regarded as the representation of the female genitalia, for instance.

In *Holy Blood, Holy Grail*, the authors Baigent, Leigh, and Lincoln note that the Priory of Sion appears to be devoted to the worship of Mary Magdalene in place of the traditional Catholic devotion to the Virgin Mary. This observation leads them to develop the theory that the main purpose of the Priory of Sion is to protect the bloodline descended from the sacred union between Jesus and Mary Magdalene, who is regarded as a highly trained priestess and of royal lineage in her own right.

Margaret Starbird, whose theories from her book *The Woman with the Alabaster Jar* also feature heavily in *The Da Vinci Code*, has spent over 10 years researching and developing the theme of the Sacred Marriage, or Hieros Gamos. Through careful study of biblical passages and systematic analysis of medieval heretical symbolism, Margaret has come to the conclusion that it's not specifically the possibility of the existence of an actual bloodline descending from Jesus and Mary Magdalene that is important, but the recognition that Jesus Himself may have celebrated the sacrament of holy matrimony in a sacred union with the Magdalene. Ironically, the revelation that the Wedding at Cana might have been an account of Jesus' own wedding would actually underscore the very principles of family and fidelity that the Church is trying to maintain within the pressures of the twenty-first-century lifestyle.

Genuine attempts to effect a more "gnostic" branch of Catholicism, incorporating sacred sexual rituals, and the restoration of the French monarchy in a manner very similar to the tenets of the Priory of Sion, can be found within a movement called the Church of Carmel, which was established in France in the early 1840s by Eugene Vintras. The belief that sex should be regarded as a "sacrament" led to accusations of Satanism against the Church of Carmel and eventually Vintras was jailed on bogus charges of fraud. After his release, a former priest in the order accused Vintras of promoting sexual orgies, and finally, in 1948, the Pope declared the order to be heretical and excommunicated all its members.

An even more direct connection with Hieros Gamos rituals and the Priory of Sion can be found in a movement known as the Brothers of Christian Doctrine, founded in 1838 by three priests, who were also brothers, by the name of Baillard. The Brothers established an important center on a former pagan site in Sion-Vaudémont in Lorraine, where the pagan love goddess Rosmerta had been Christianized as a Black Madonna in 994.

Also known as the Brothers of Notre-Dame of Sion, this modern movement appears to have been inspired by a genuine chivalric order, the Order of Notre-Dame of Sion, founded in 1393 by Ferri I de Vaudémont. Ferri's son, Ferri II, married Iolande de Bar, the daughter of Good King René d'Anjou, both of whom are cited as Grand Masters of the Priory of Sion in the Dossiers Secrets. At this marriage, the Priory of Sion and the Order of Notre-Dame of Sion are thought to have merged.

Five hundred years later, the Baillard brothers' version of Catholicism, emphasizing the Holy Spirit and sacred sexuality, attracted a great deal of support, especially among the aristocracy, but it was also suppressed, in 1852, amid predictable accusations that the movement was celebrating Black Masses. After this, any attempts to incorporate sacred sexuality within Catholicism went underground, where a multitude of genuine—and not-so-genuine—esoteric orders have proliferated.

Today, attempts are being made to ascertain whether Jesus really was married to Mary Magdalene. Whether it can be proved that the marriage of Jesus was an actual historical fact or whether these attempts are inspired by a deep primal human need to restore the Divine Feminine to one of the world's oldest patriarchal religions remains to be seen.

See also: Black Madonnas; Dossiers Secrets; Priory of Sion.

oly Blood, Holy Grail

The international best-seller, from which a good deal of the background of *The Da Vinci Code* is drawn. Written by Michael Baigent, Richard Leigh, and Henry Lincoln, and first published in 1982, *HBHG*, as it is affectionately referred to, is generally considered to be the "bible" of the Priory of Sion.

Although today's Priory of Sion researchers continue to dispute the veracity of the historical information contained within the book, there is a general agreement overall that *Holy Blood, Holy Grail* has, for better or for worse, been singularly responsible for unleashing revolutionary religious and historical concepts that had never been publicly examined before. Furthermore, *HBHG* is the only English-language book among the veritable cottage industry of Priory of Sion books that was written by authors who have actually had firsthand access to a supposed Grand Master of the secret society itself.

Despite the controversy, *HBHG* provides an invaluable layman's introduction to the convoluted historical development behind the esoteric, Gnostic, and chivalric mindset. Piquing our interest with the tale of a mysterious treasure at Rennes-le-Château in the south of France, Baigent, Leigh, and Lincoln expand the quest throughout the book to include a romantic examination of Catharism, an early heretical version of Christianity, before moving onto a history of the Knights Templar. Because the secret Priory archives, the Dossiers Secrets, claim that the Priory of Sion was the hidden force behind the formation of the Knights Templar, a large part of *Holy Blood, Holy Grail* dwells on Grand Master Pierre Plantard's version of the development of the order after the split from the Templars, embroidering a colorful account of how kings and internationally renowned scientists, intellectuals, and artists, including Leonardo Da Vinci, Sir Isaac Newton, Victor Hugo, Claude Debussy, and Jean Cocteau, gently guided the course of humanity over the past 1,000 years.

However, the most intriguing aspect of the unraveling of the Priory of Sion's history is the authors' personal interaction with the enigmatic Grand Master, Pierre Plantard. He leads the authors on a wild-goose chase through obscure documents and locations throughout France in order to verify minute, and sometimes completely meaningless, details in an attempt to confirm whether the Priory of Sion is actually genuine or simply the product of an ingenious and elaborate hoax. As Baigent, Leigh, and Lincoln come to grips with a myriad number of esoteric and historical codes, the quest is transformed into a multidimensional psychological chess game, which is exactly the aspect of the search that continues successfully to hook in every Priory of Sion researcher to this very day.

Finally, in an attempt to synthesize the overload of cryptic and historical data, Baigent, Leigh, and Lincoln embark on the mind-blowing quantum leap that is at the root of *Holy Blood, Holy Grail*'s reputation as an "explosively controversial" best-seller—the bloodline of Jesus and Mary Magdalene.

The seed is germinated by Pierre Plantard during his first meeting with the authors. During this meeting, Plantard stated definitively that the Priory of Sion held the lost treasure of the Temple of Jerusalem and that it would be returned to Israel when the time was right. But then he stressed that the historical, financial, and even political value of this treasure was incidental, emphasizing that the real significance of the treasure was "spiritual" and that part of the spiritual aspect of the treasure consisted of a secret, the revelation of which would cause major social change in the Western world.

With only this small, tantalizing clue in hand, coupled with Plantard's own personal obsession with intricate genealogies and his alleged descent from the Merovingian kings, Baigent, Leigh, and Lincoln devote the final third section of *Holy Blood, Holy Grail* to setting out their theory that the real secret purpose of the Priory of Sion was to guard the holy bloodline descending from the offspring of Jesus and Mary Magdalene. Their logical process is so thorough and so convincing that most readers automatically assume that this is indeed the case, but in actual fact Pierre Plantard never confirmed this hypothesis, which was entirely developed by the authors of *HBHG* as a result of their intensive detective work.

The irony of this conundrum unfolds in Baigent, Leigh, and Lincoln's follow-up book, *The Messianic Legacy*, as the trio continue to relate the ongoing saga of their personal experiences with the Priory of Sion. The authors' dilemma is underscored as they wait with bated breath for Plantard's reaction to the French manuscript of *Holy Blood, Holy Grail*, which they had submitted to him as a courtesy for his comments. Plantard's response to their bloodline theory was disappointingly ambivalent, on the one hand noncommittally observing that there was no reliable evidence to prove that the Merovingian bloodline was descended from Jesus, while on the other hand acknowledging that the Merovingians did indeed derive from the royal line of David. Furthermore, Plantard's comments regarding Mary Magdalene's role in the bloodline dynasty were conspicuous by their absence.

Nevertheless, despite Plantard's reluctance to actively endorse the Priory of Sion's part in Jesus' and Mary Magdalene's bloodline theory, so seductive is Baigent, Leigh, and Lincoln's research that, over the course of the past 20 years, *Holy Blood, Holy Grail* has been the inspiration behind an entire catalog of books, including *The Da Vinci Code*, which have been produced to examine the alternative histories of a never-ending stream of esoteric mysteries, secret societies, and chivalric orders that inevitably claim their own descent from the bloodline of Jesus and Mary Magdalene.

Dan Brown himself pays specific homage to *Holy Blood, Holy Grail* when his character Leigh Teabing, an amalgam of Richard Leigh's and Michael Baigent's names, specifically cites the book during his explanation of the Priory of Sion to Sophie at Château Villette: "...This [book] caused quite a stir in the nineteen eighties. To my taste, the authors made some dubious leaps of faith in their analysis, but their fundamental premise is sound, and to their credit, they finally brought the idea of Christ's bloodline into the mainstream."

However, experienced researchers of the Priory of Sion are aware that *Holy Blood, Holy Grail* isn't actually the first book to fuse Plantard's history of the Priory of Sion with the Sacred Feminine and the bloodline of Jesus and Mary Magdalene. A good two years before *HBHG* was published, the well-known astrologer Liz Greene released a novel about Nostradamus called *The Dreamer of the Vine*, which interwove the now-familiar elements of the Priory history into Nostradamus's life story. In hindsight, *The Dreamer of the Vine* appears to be an astonishingly prescient premonition of the same elements that caused so much controversy when *Holy Blood, Holy Grail* burst onto the scene in 1982. But when one begins to dig a little bit deeper, to discover that Liz Greene is actually the sister of Richard Leigh and was at the time the girlfriend of Michael Baigent, a cunning pattern begins to emerge...

So, did the authors of *Holy Blood, Holy Grail* really just "happen" to evolve the Jesus and Mary Magdalene bloodline concept during the course of their discussions with Pierre Plantard, or was this the destination of the book all along? If the latter is the case, were Baigent and Leigh privy to some long suppressed inside information before the first words of *Holy Blood, Holy Grail* were ever set down on a page? And if so, who was really navigating whom... and are we still on course?

73

Holy Grail

The central theme and ultimate point of Dan Brown's book is an understanding of what the Holy Grail represents.

In the various versions of the legend, the Holy Grail has been depicted as a cup or chalice, a relic containing the blood of Christ, a silver platter, a cauldron of plenty, a stone from heaven, a dish, a fish, a dove, a sword, a spear, a lance, a secret book, manna from heaven, a severed head, a blinding white light, a table, and much else besides.

The quest not only to understand the Grail but also to find it is one that has been with us for over 1,000 years and is deeply ingrained in the psyche of modern man. The Grail has been presented in many possible forms from medieval times onward, and the quest for it has engaged the minds of many. So what do we know of its origins?

The conventional view of the Grail is that it is the chalice that once held the blood of Christ and that Joseph of Arimathea brought it to Britain. Joseph is believed to have taken it to Glastonbury in southern England, since when its whereabouts have become shrouded in mystery. Legend holds that this cup or Grail was used at the Last Supper as well as being used to collect the blood of Christ at the Crucifixion, though different stories have different characters collecting the blood—some have Joseph of Arimathea, some have Nicodemus, and some have Mary Magdalene. The legends continued through the centuries, reaching a peak in the Middle Ages.

The earliest Grail romances were written down in the twelfth and thirteenth centuries, with a great number written between 1190 and 1240, though the story seems to have had an earlier oral tradition. These dates coincide with the rise of the Knights Templar in medieval Europe. The romances themselves were written mainly by monks from the Cistercian and Benedictine orders, with many of the tales and romances having a distinctly Templar-based theme running through them.

Early on, it becomes obvious that there is no such thing as a single Grail story, or a typical one. Most of the Grail romances don't even agree with each other. One of the earliest known Grail stories is that written by Chrétien de Troyes, with his *Le Conte du Graal*, composed around 1190. It is in this tale that we are first introduced to the character of Perceval, the guileless knight and archetypal fool of the Grail stories. Perceval first sees what he believes to be the Grail at a great feast at the Fisher King's castle, along with a sword that is broken and many other strange sights and events. The Fisher King is a strange figure who appears in the Grail and Arthurian legends, but whose mysterious character is not fully understood. It seems that Chrétien died before finishing his intriguing story, and it was partly completed by later hands in versions that are called *The Continuations*. These versions add embellishments and color to the original story, adding elements that were to become standard in later tales.

Two other Grail stories written around 1200 are Robert

de Boron's tales, *Joseph d'Arimathie* and *Merlin*. These tales are given a new Christian slant, showing the quest as a spiritual one by the knights, rather than a story of courtly honor or for the hand of a fair maiden. It is here, in the early part of the thirteenth century, that Robert de Boron's tales are linked closely with the Arthurian legends that were popular at the time, with both Sir Gawain and Sir Galahad featuring in tales of the era. It was also at this time that the best-known story in the English-speaking world was written down. *The Queste*, featuring Sir Galahad, son of Sir Lancelot, is the basis for Sir Thomas Mallory's brilliant fifteenth-century epic, *Le Morte d'Arthur*. This work, more than any other, is responsible for the modern-day perception of not only the Arthurian legends but also the Grail romances. Mallory's book has had as big an impact on the minds of man over the past 500 years as any you care to mention.

In around 1205, a Bavarian poet named Wolfram von Eschenbach composed the poem "Parzival." In it he tells of the hero's quest first told by Chrétien de Troyes, the difference being that in Wolfram's work the Grail becomes a stone. Not any old stone, though: this one is a luminous stone that has fallen from heaven. It is the first time that the Grail is not described as a cup, as in the other romances. Wolfram's stone is guarded by knights, called Templeisen, obviously meant to be Templar Knights. In Wolfram's story, young Parzival is on a quest to the Grail castle, here called the Mount of Salvation, when he meets on the way a wise old man called Trevrizent, with whom he stays for 15 days. It turns out that the old man is Parzival's uncle, who tells him that the story of the Grail came from a wise man called Kyot of Provence. According to various scholars, Kyot was a real person, in the guise of one Guiot de Provins, thus giving the story a basis in reality. Trevrizent claims that Kyot encountered the Grail story in a book written in a strange, heathen language in Toledo in Spain. This "heathen language" was most probably Arabic, used in Toledo by the Moors of North Africa. Trevrizent goes on to tell Parzival that this book was written by a man called Flegetanis, whose mother was a Jewess of the lineage of Solomon and whose father seems to have been an astrologer.

The story of Parzival as told by Wolfram is one of purity and judgment. Only the pure of heart and mind can attain the Grail, and only God can judge who should achieve this. Parzival eventually returns to the Grail castle in the story, asks the Fisher King the right question, and thus heals the dying king. Parzival then becomes the Grail king himself, and the cycle continues.

The idea that the Grail is a metaphor for the bloodline of Christ and the origins of his family lineage is a relatively modern one, though many of the modern authors on this subject would have us believe that this truth was known through history by a select few artisans and wise men, who encoded this idea into works of art and architecture throughout the ages. The idea of the Priory of Sion and its Grand Masters is a classic example of this.

The stories of the original use of the Holy Grail—collecting Christ's blood at the Crucifixion—definitely connect the precious blood of Christ with the Grail and may well be a metaphor for the actual bloodline of the Christian Messiah. Intertwined within this theory is the idea that Christ allegedly married Mary Magdalene before his death, and that she bore him a child. The family line of Christ supposedly, therefore, continues to this day, with the Grail becoming the "vine" through which the family of Christ is linked with the Merovingian kings of France. The hypothesis is that after the Crucifixion Mary Magdalene traveled to France with their child, and that intermarriage with the Frankish tribes of a descendant of Christ produced the Merovingian kings. This idea was first popularized by the authors Michael Baigent, Henry Lincoln, and Richard Leigh in their best-selling book *Holy Blood, Holy Grail*, first published over 20 years ago but now enjoying something of a renaissance because of the popularity of *The Da Vinci Code*, which draws much of its background information from the work.

See also: Holy Blood, Holy Grail; Joseph of Arimathea; Knights Templar; Mary Magdalene.

Isis

Jacques Saunière, the character in *The Da Vinci Code* who is the curator at the Louvre Museum, Paris, is portrayed as an expert in goddess worship. In this capacity he has added many statues of Isis with her son Horus to the museum's collection. When a description of Teabing's house is given, we learn that he has an Isis statue on his mantelpiece.

Isis is the most powerful ancient Egyptian goddess—the universal goddess. Isis is the mother of the god Horus, and hence symbolic mother of the king, and wife and sister of Osiris, the god of the underworld. She is called "Great in Magic" and is praised for her skills in healing and promoting fertility. Her high status and her role as mother of the king is highlighted by the throne hieroglyph used to denote her name and which she is often depicted wearing on her head. In her various roles, Isis was shown in a number of manifestations; as mother she was sometimes represented as the "great sow of Heliopolis," or as the Isis-cow, the mother of the sacred Apis bull of Memphis. As Hathor, which means "House of Horus" (i.e. the womb of Isis), she is shown wearing a sun disk that rests between a pair of large cow horns. The symbol of Isis is the *tyet*, or "knot of Isis," which resembles an ankh sign but with the crossbars turned downward instead of standing out horizontally. The *tyet* is thought to represent the padding used for a menstrual period, and, indeed, a spell from the *Book of the Dead* states that *tyet* amulets were to be made from red jasper, a type of quartz.

The origins of Isis are obscure. The first mention of her comes in the fourth and fifth dynasties (2492–2181 BC) in the Pyramid Texts, the oldest written collection of Egyptian religious, funerary, and magical literature. However, their obvious oral nature and archaic language suggest that they originate from a much earlier time and perhaps date from the second and third dynasties (2890—2613 BC). In theology, she was the daughter of Geb and Nut and sister to Osiris, Seth, Nephthys, and Thoth. The tradition states that Seth, jealous of his brother's kingship of Egypt, murdered Osiris on the banks of the Nile in the north of Egypt. When Isis discovers that her beloved brother is dead, she is inconsolable and searches all Egypt to find his body. At last Isis manages to retrieve his body, and through her excellent magical and healing skills she is able to revive her brother sufficiently to have intercourse with him and conceive a son, Horus. This she does so that Horus can avenge Osiris's murder. Isis's main aim now is to protect her son so that he can claim his birthright: the throne of Egypt that has been usurped by Seth.

Isis achieves her goal through due legal procedure, taking her son's case through the courts of the gods—the Broad Hall of Geb—where she is "clever of tongue" in her pleas for her son. So that Seth himself will proclaim in favor of Horus, Isis manages to trick her brother. Disguised as a beautiful stranger, Isis meets with Seth and recounts to him how her husband was murdered and his land and cattle stolen, leaving her son fatherless, homeless, and without means of livelihood. She asks Seth to help her retrieve her son's rightful property. Seth is disgusted by the unjust way in which her son has been treated, and when Isis reveals her true identity Seth is humiliated before the gods. After a number of similar encounters, the gods finally decide against Seth, stating that Horus was to be the ruler of the living and that Osiris was to rule over the dead. Thus, Isis is instrumental in ensuring that Horus became rightful ruler of Egypt, and in this role she is seen as the protector of kingship, with every pharaoh described as the living Horus.

The protection Isis gave to her son Horus while he was growing up is the reason for her association with the protection of children from harm. Accordingly, there are many medicinal and magical spells in her name that can be used to cure and protect children from such things as burns or scorpion or snake bites.

Isis is renowned for her wisdom and guile, and she was considered "more clever than a million gods." Through her skills and cunning she is able to obtain the secret name of the god Re and, furthermore, to get Re's permission to pass on this knowledge to Horus and hence to the living pharaohs themselves. To find out anybody's secret name was a very powerful tool for an ancient Egyptian, as it meant having magical power over that person. To have a god's secret name meant indescribable power.

There are many stories attached to Isis underlining her power of healing, fertility, wisdom, and protection, and these factors, along with her close association with Egyptian kingship, meant that her cult centers and temples can be found throughout Egypt. The most famous Isis temple was situated on the island of Philae in southern Egypt and dates mainly to the Greco-Roman period (380 BC–AD 30). By the time of Cleopatra (51–30 BC), the Isis cult was the official religion of Egypt.

Her universal appeal enabled her cult to spread beyond the confines of Egypt and out into the Mediterranean world and beyond. Temples to Isis were located as far as Athens, Pompeii, Paris, and even London. Her cult, which had changed slightly as it left Egypt, became so popular with the people of Rome that the Senate, fearing an uprising by the masses, ordered the Temple of Isis and Serapis (Osiris) to be destroyed, although the threat was never carried out. Despite Julius Caesar abolishing the cult, it continued to flourish. Notwithstanding later persecutions and expulsions, Isis became the center of a mystery cult that was extremely popular and spread throughout the Hellenistic world and the Roman Empire.

The popularity of Isis stemmed from her universal appeal as mother, wife, healer, protector, and savior. This appeal became so widespread that in later periods it even rivaled Christianity for dominance. In around AD 140, Apuleius wrote about the initiation ceremony into the Isis cult in his book *Metamorphoses*. He also described Isis as the eternal savior, terms reminiscent of Christianity. In fact, many aspects of the early Christian Church have their origins in the Isis cult, such as the iconography of the Madonna and Child, certain attributes and titles of the Virgin Mary, the forgiveness of sins through repentance, baptism by water, the redemption and salvation through the divine, and an eternal afterlife.

See also: Goddess Worship; Louvre; Osiris; Saunière, Jacques.

Joseph of Arimathea

Once Sophie Neveu has made the discovery that the supposed bloodline of Christ and Mary Magdalene is linked to her own family story, she has a lot to absorb. Teabing, the Grail scholar, explains the theory to her that Joseph of Arimathea helped Mary escape to France after the Crucifixion.

Joseph of Arimathea is described in all four Gospels as the man who obtained the body of Christ for burial after His Crucifixion (Matthew 27: 59, 60; Mark 15: 46; Luke 23: 53; John 19: 38–40). At Joseph of Arimathea's expense, the body of Christ was interred in Joseph's rock tomb, where, aided by the Pharisee priest Nicodemus, it was wrapped in fine linen and spices.

The Gospels provide only a brief description of Joseph of Arimathea, so that we know little about the man apart from the fact that he was wealthy and a secret disciple of Jesus (John 19: 38). Luke (23: 50) adds that Joseph of Arimathea was a member of the Sanhedrin ruling council, which suggests that he held a position of some authority. It appears that Joseph of Arimathea, who was considered a "good and upright man" (Luke 23: 50), had not agreed with the Sanhedrin's sentencing of Jesus. According to Matthew (27: 57–60) and Mark (15: 43–5), Joseph of Arimathea personally asked Pontius Pilate for the dead body of Christ, suggesting that Joseph was sufficiently powerful to be granted an audience with the Roman governor of Judea. Under Jewish custom, it was the duty of the closest male relative to arrange burial, and so it has been suggested that Joseph of Arimathea was the brother of Jesus (see Graham Phillips, *The Marian Conspiracy*), although Eastern tradition believes him to be the uncle of the Virgin Mary.

Some non-canonical texts shed a little more light on Joseph. The Gospel of Peter mentions that he was actually a personal friend of Pontius Pilate, and the Gospel of Nicodemus refers to the burial of Jesus and states that afterward the Jewish elders imprisoned Joseph of Arimathea. While Joseph was in prison, the risen Jesus appeared to him and miraculously transported him to his home, where Jesus told him to remain for 40 days. The Jewish elders were amazed to find out that Joseph had escaped and that the locks and seal on his cell had not been broken or tampered with. Realizing that they were dealing with an exalted person, they wrote Joseph a letter of apology and requested him to meet with them in Jerusalem. At the meeting, Joseph explained exactly what had taken place and informed the Jewish elders that others had also risen at the same time as Jesus. The Narrative of Joseph also confirms the story of Joseph's imprisonment. The Passing of Mary is supposedly a Gospel written by Joseph of Arimathea himself, who after the Crucifixion attended the Virgin Mary.

Compared with the sparseness of information found on Joseph of Arimathea in the Gospels, he features heavily in the apocryphal texts, later legends, and Arthurian romances. In these accounts, it is said that Joseph was a tin merchant who brought Jesus to England in His youth, that he was the founder of Christianity in Britain, and that he was the guardian of the Holy Grail. That Joseph of Arimathea, a small player in the New Testament, should be linked to Britain is somewhat surprising, but a long tradition associates him with Cornwall and Somerset. These traditions state that Joseph once brought the young Jesus with him on a tin trading trip. If Joseph was familiar with Britain at this time, then it is understandable why Philip the Apostle later sent him there from Gaul.

Although the official founder of Christianity in Britain was St Augustine in AD 597, non-canonical sources and later accounts relate that Joseph of Arimathea had actually arrived in Britain in either AD 37 or 63. The narratives state that Joseph fled Judaea with a number of others, usually the Apostle Philip, Lazarus, Mary Magdalene, Martha, Mary of Bethany, and others. At Marseilles, Lazarus and Mary Magdalene stayed behind while the rest of the group traveled into Gaul, farther north in modern France. Philip the Apostle then sent Joseph of Arimathea and either 11 or 12 others (depending on the text) to Britain in order to preach. The sea journey took Joseph to the West Country, where the local king, Arviragus, granted Joseph and his companions some land on the White Island. It was here that Joseph and his companions built a wattle church, the Vetusta Ecclesia, dedicated to the Virgin Mary. It is generally accepted that this is the present site of Glastonbury (compare Graham Phillips, who believes this is Anglesey) and that the Benedictine monastery of Glastonbury now occupies the site where the church stood. Most of these details can be found in *The Antiquity of the Church at Glastonbury*, written in the twelfth century by William of Malmesbury, as well as the twelfth-century *Chronicle of the Antiquities of the Church of Glastonbury* by John of Glastonbury. However, an earlier account of Joseph's part in bringing Christianity to Britain was provided in the sixth century in *The History of the Franks* by Gregory of Tours.

Another part of the story that relates to Joseph and the early Christian community at Glastonbury concerns the hawthorn bush supposedly planted by Joseph. While stopping to rest on Wearyall Hill, Joseph drove his staff into the ground, at which point a hawthorn bush grew. The staff that Joseph carried with him had been grown from the crown of thorns that Jesus wore at His Crucifixion. The hawthorn, which is still in Glastonbury, flowers in May and at Christmas and is referred to as the Holy Thorn. However, the earliest mention of this comes in *The Lyfe of Joseph of Arimathia* written in 1520, with later additions to the tale surfacing in 1677 and 1716.

Probably the most famous myth that surrounds Joseph of Arimathea concerns his guardianship of the Holy Grail. In these stories, the Holy Grail is usually associated with the cup used by Jesus at the Last Supper and in which Joseph caught a few drops of Jesus' blood during the Crucifixion. The first mention of this, albeit rudimentary, comes in *The Life of St Mary Magdalene* by Rabanus Maurus (776–856). In this, Joseph of Arimathea is closely linked with the legendary Isle of Avalon, supposedly in Somerset, where he is buried beneath the church he founded. It is also stated that buried with him were two silver vessels that contained the blood and sweat of Jesus.

In the medieval period, many Grail stories were in circulation, notably Robert de Boron's *Joseph d'Arimathie*. In this, Robert de Boron relates how Jesus is speared in the side while on the cross, with Joseph catching some of the blood in the cup used at the Last Supper. For his association with Jesus, the Jewish authorities imprison Joseph, during which Jesus miraculously appears to him and teaches him the "mysteries of the Grail," though it is not made clear what these mysteries were. After 42 years' imprisonment, Joseph is freed, and along with a group of Christians travels to a foreign country, where a round table is constructed to symbolize the Last Supper. However, one place is never used: the place for Judas. Subsequently, a location is sought to house the Holy Grail, and this is found in the Vale of Avalon (Glastonbury), where a church is built for this purpose.

Other stories of this kind were very popular in the medieval period, such as *Grand St Grail* (1200), *Parzival* (1207) by Wolfram von Eschenbach, *Queste del St Graal* (1210), *Perlesvaus* (1225), and, most important, Sir Thomas Malory's *Le Morte d'Arthur* (1485). In Malory's story, Joseph of Arimathea is the true guardian of the Holy Grail and the ancestor of Arthur, Lancelot, and Galahad.

See also: Holy Grail; Mary Magdalene; Teabing, Leigh.

Knights Templar

The earliest order of military monks, the Knights Templar were formed in 1118 when a knight of Champagne, a certain Hughes de Payens, and eight companions bound themselves with a perpetual vow taken in the presence of the patriarch, or ruler, of Jerusalem. Initially, they survived on alms and were known as the Poor Knights of Christ.

The Knights Templar are mentioned throughout *The Da Vinci Code*, in association with either the Holy Grail or with finding the so-called treasure of the temple of Jerusalem.

The Knights soon adopted the famed white habit, which came from the Cistercians, adding to it a red cross. They vowed initially to defend the roads to the Holy Land for the new pilgrims who flocked to Jerusalem from Europe after the First Crusade. Soon, however, the Knights became a power base in their own right, with large numbers joining the new order, despite the seeming austerity of their monastic rule.

The Church at this time were very much in favor of the Knights. Their property was exempt from tax, favors of all kinds were heaped on them, they were not subject to jurisdiction, and didn't even have to pay the ecclesiastical tithes that were rife at the time. This in turn led to a growing antipathy toward the order from certain sections of the secular clergy. Their strength was bolstered by an array of impressive castles built in the Holy Land; these served as both places of military campaign and as chapels to which the warrior monks could retreat.

The name Knights Templar seems to allude to the fact that they had their historical headquarters in Jerusalem at the Dome of the Rock, on the Temple Mount, which they renamed Templum Domini. Many believed this place to be the site of the legendary Temple of Jerusalem built by Solomon, with its purported treasure. Subsequent churches and strongholds built by the Templars were modeled on this site, such as Temple Church in London.

The Templars enjoyed the patronage of Bernard of Clairvaux, the founder of the Cistercian order, who championed their cause to all who would listen within the Church. As a result they received several Papal Bulls, or notices, that empowered them to raise taxes and tithes in areas that they controlled. This in turn gave them instant power and authority.

One of the first international banking systems was set up by the order, and wealthy knights and landowners would often leave the bulk of their wealth in the safe hands of the order—for a fee, of course. The Templars eventually owned extensive properties in both Europe and the Middle East; at one point they were even in line to own the Spanish kingdom of Aragon after fighting in a Spanish campaign.

The order gained a reputation as being secretive and obsessed with rituals, and this reputation, along with the Knights' huge financial and military power, was probably the reason for their downfall in 1307. On Friday October 13, 1307 (the origin of the idea of bad luck falling on Friday 13), a substantial number of the Knights Templar in France were arrested by Philip the Fair of France. Many were tortured and executed, and others were forced into admitting that the order practiced heretical acts, including the worship of Baphomet, an idol with a goat's head. Pope Clement V issued a Papal Bull dissolving the order, and officially it ceased to exist. However, it would seem that remnants of the order remained, especially in Scotland, where Robert the Bruce, already excommunicated by the Church, welcomed the order into his country. Some have speculated that a division of Knights Templar may have entered the fray on the side of the Scots at the Battle of Bannockburn, where a 10,000-strong army led by the Bruce managed to rout a 25,000-strong contingent of Englishmen in 1314.

Speculation has grown ever since the order was disbanded that they had found a great treasure beneath the Temple Mount. Stories persist of many chests, filled with books and documents that they secreted away from France on the eve of their downfall—many place the destination of these documents in England or Scotland. Theories abound that they found not only great wealth beneath the Temple Mount but also the Ark of the Covenant and even the Holy Grail itself—information that would be damaging to the Church. Rumors and legends also associate the Templars with Rosslyn Chapel and with Rennes-le-Château in the south of France, a place central to the story of the Priory of Sion.

In the end, the Templars were simply victims of their own success. Their power and position made them extremely unpopular within certain sections of the Church, and this led to their eventual downfall. This, coupled with the fact that King Philip the Fair of France wanted his hands on their banking organization and network, meant they would face inevitable ruin.

Did the Templars protect the knowledge of the Holy Grail and what it was? Probably not, but unless the treasure is found we will never know.

See also: Baphomet; Bernard of Clairvaux, St; Holy Grail; Priory of Sion.

Langdon, Robert

Lead character in *The Da Vinci Code*, Langdon also features in Dan Brown's book *Angels and Demons*. Robert Langdon is supposedly Professor of Religious Symbology at Harvard University and the author of over a dozen books. The fictitious character of Langdon also has a fictitious job title—"symbology" seems to be an amalgam word, made up of "symbolism" and "cryptology," with Harvard University having no such post as Professor of Religious Symbology. However, the work carried out by Robert Langdon is touched on by two real-life Harvard professors, Nicholas P. Constas, who works on the theological study of icons and iconography, and Kimberley C. Patton, who has interests in the study of dream interpretation and the iconography of sacrifice as well as funerary cults.

The fictitious Robert Langdon has a real website: www.robertlangdon.com.

Last Supper, The

For many scholars and art historians, Leonardo's *The Last Supper* is seen as the world's greatest painting. In *The Da Vinci Code*, Brown highlights some possible symbolic characterizations within the painting when, at Leigh Teabing's house, Sophie is introduced to the notion that Leonardo encoded a great secret into his masterpiece.

The Last Supper is a fresco painted on a wall of the refectory of Santa Maria delle Grazie in Milan, Italy. Even in Leonardo's own day, this was considered his most famous and best work. The wall painting was executed between 1495 and 1497, but within 20 years was already starting to deteriorate, according to contemporary records. It measures some 15 by 29 feet and is painted in a thick layer of egg tempera on top of dry plaster. Beneath the main coat of paint lies a rough compositional structure, sketched in a reddish color in a manner that predates his usual use of cartoons as a preparatory tool.

It is thought that the painting was probably commissioned by Ludovico Sforza, Duke of Milan, in whose court Leonardo was to find fame, and not by the monks of Santa Maria delle Grazie.

The theme of the painting is the point at which Jesus has just announced that one of His followers will betray Him. We know this from the work of Pacioli, who states this fact in the third chapter of his book, *Divina Proportione*. This actual announcement and the different reactions of the Apostles around the table is the moment that Leonardo chose to freeze in time. To capture the most lifelike expressions, Leonardo studied the poses, facial expressions, and physiognomies of many of his contemporaries, which he later incorporated into the painting. The identities of the individual Apostles is a much-argued subject, but based on inscriptions on a copy of the painting in Lugano, they are, from left to right: Bartholomew, James the Younger, Andrew, Judas, Peter, John, Thomas, James the Elder, Philip, Matthew, Thaddeus, and Simon the Zealot.

Many art historians believe that the composition can be seen as an iconographical interpretation of the Eucharist, because Jesus is pointing with both hands to the bread and the wine on the table. Others say that only the betrayal announcement is being portrayed. Most art historians do agree, however, that the ideal position from which to view the work is some 13 to 15 feet above floor level and between 26 and 33 feet away. Some have claimed that the composition and its perspective system are based on a musical canon of proportion, though this has been disputed recently.

The Last Supper is unique among all paintings of this scene in that the Apostles show an amazing array of emotions and reactions to the news that one of their number will betray Jesus. No other painting of the Last Supper comes anywhere near this kind of detail and composition.

So what of the mysteries supposedly encoded within this masterpiece? In their book *The Templar Revelation*, Clive Prince and Lynn Picknett claim that there are several elements to the structure of the work that betray an encoded symbolism.

First, they believe that the figure to the right of Jesus (left as we look) is not actually John but a female figure. She is dressed in contrasting colored clothing to Jesus and is leaning in an opposite direction to the central figure of Jesus, thus forming a V with the space and an M with their bodies.

Secondly, there appears to be a disembodied hand, clutching a knife, close to the figure of Peter. Prince and Picknett claim that this hand cannot belong to any other figure in the painting.

Thirdly, immediately to the left of Jesus (right as we look), Thomas is confronting Jesus with the upraised finger gesture, or, as the authors call it, the John gesture.

And finally it is claimed that the character of Thaddeus is actually a self-portrait of Leonardo, who is turning his back on Jesus.

Let us take each point in turn. A close examination of the painting reveals that the character to the right of Jesus (left as we look) does indeed have feminine or effeminate features. Prince and Picknett even claim that the folds in the tunic of the figure reveal the outline of female breasts. Certainly, Leonardo was not averse to giving feminine attributes and features to several of his male painted figures. For example, a close inspection of his famous painting of John the Baptist shows him with an almost hermaphroditic set of features and pale hairless skin. But what of the fact that in *The Last Supper* Jesus and the John/female figure seem to lean in opposite directions, forming a natural V with the space between their bodies and therefore an M when you include the line of their bodies? Does this have any symbolic relevance? Prince and Picknett argue that this unusual alignment of the figures, coupled with the feminine features of "John," show us that this figure actually represents Mary Magdalene herself, with the V sign being the symbol of the Sacred Feminine and the M sign standing for Mary/Magdalene. Clearly, whether one agrees with this hypothesis or not, this is an original and exciting interpretation.

So now we come to the famous disembodied hand. Whose hand is visible on the left of the table, close to the figure of Peter? Why is it grasping a dagger or knife in such a menacing manner? Another strange feature is that Peter's left hand seems to be cutting across the neck of the feminine figure in a threatening gesture. What was Leonardo trying to tell us about Peter here?

On closer inspection, and seeing the painting at close quarters, it seems obvious that the hand and knife in question actually belong to Peter himself, who is twisting his right hand around and resting it on his side, albeit rather awkwardly and unnaturally. As for Peter's left hand cutting across the neck of the John/Mary figure, another interpretation is that Peter is simply resting his left hand on the figure's shoulder. It appears that the debate will continue for some time yet.

As for Thomas, immediately to the left of Jesus (right as we look), he is indeed raising his left hand index finger in a seemingly threatening manner. This John gesture, as Prince and Picknett call it, is evident in a whole host of works by Leonardo and indeed by other painters of the time. In brief it is said to represent an underground stream of knowledge and wisdom, which has its belief structures based on the idea that John the Baptist played a far more important role than is generally ascertained from the Scriptures. For those interested in a full explanation I recommend a reading of *The Templar Revelation*.

The Thaddeus figure does seem to bear a resemblance to the real Leonardo, as can be seen by Leonardo's famous self-portrait. In many of Leonardo's paintings that involve Jesus or the Holy Family, there is the recurring theme of at least one figure with its back to the central character—see *Adoration of the Magi* as an example.

The recently finished and highly controversial restoration of *The Last Supper* has revealed many new and exciting features of this amazing painting. There do indeed seem to be hidden messages and forgotten symbolism in this and many other Leonardo compositions, though what they relate to is unclear and this had led to much supposition and theorizing. However, more needs to be done in this field in future if we can even remotely begin to unravel the mind of the master.

See also: Adoration of the Magi; Leonardo Da Vinci.

Leonardo Da Vinci

The presence of Leonardo Da Vinci is felt throughout the novel as a powerful influence on Jacques Saunière, the man whose murder starts the story. Several works of the artist are used as clues for his granddaughter, Sophie Neveu, to follow, and the cryptex, or physical puzzle, that she uses is said to be a design by Da Vinci.

Born in 1452 near the small Tuscan hill village of Vinci, Leonardo was to become a true Renaissance man. Renowned as a painter, sculptor, architect, musician, engineer, and scientist, Leonardo was a man of rare genius and ability who depicted in his drawings such subjects as flying machines and anatomical studies, all carried out with consummate scientific precision and artistry.

As the illegitimate son of a Florentine notary and a peasant girl, it is assumed that Leonardo spent most of his childhood with his father's family in Vinci. It was here that it's believed his enduring interest and fascination with nature and the natural world began. He showed a great artistic talent from an early age and was said to be a precocious and charming child.

In 1466, Leonardo moved to Florence and entered the workshop of Verrocchio, the Florentine sculptor and painter (real name Andrea di Michele di Francesco di Cioni), who was a leading figure in the early Renaissance, his workshop being a magnet for aspiring young artists and sculptors in Florence. While at the Verrocchio workshop, Leonardo came into contact with such artists as Ghirlandaio and Botticelli. The former was an artist of excellent technical ability who tended to depict many prominent Florentine personalities within a religious narrative, and the latter was a painter who became one of the greatest colorists in Florence, and also one of the favorite painters of the Medici family, going on to help decorate the Sistine Chapel in the Vatican under Pope Sixtus IV. Leonardo was undoubtedly influenced by both of these brilliant painters and their work over the course of his stay in the workshop. In 1472, Leonardo was registered in the painters' guild, and in 1481 he was commissioned by the monks of San Donato a Scopeto to paint his *Adoration of the*

Magi (now in the Uffizi), the magnificent but unfinished masterpiece showing signs of his burgeoning mature style that would permeate his later works.

In 1482 Leonardo entered the court of Ludovico Sforza in Milan, remaining for the next 16 years. Sforza, Duke of Milan, was known as "the Moor" because of his swarthy complexion. Along with his wife Este, he held a sumptuous court, spending huge sums of money patronizing the arts. It was in this atmosphere that Leonardo started fully to develop his genius. He took an interest in town planning during the severe plagues of 1484 and 1485, an interest that he was to revive in his later years in France. Also during this time, Leonardo had contact with the brilliant architect Bramante, whose work seems to have inspired Leonardo's designs and drawings for the elevations of domed churches and buildings in general. In 1490, Leonardo was employed as the consulting engineer on the restoration of the cathedral of Pavia.

In 1483, Leonardo, along with his pupil of the time, Ambrogio de Predis, was commissioned to paint the now-famous *Madonna of the Rocks*. The commission came from an organization known as the Confraternity of the Immaculate Conception, which originally wanted a single painting to adorn the centerpiece of a triptych for the altar of the chapel of their church, San Francesco Grande, in Milan. However, the first version of the painting, which today hangs in the Louvre in Paris, was superseded by a second version, now in the National Gallery, London, which was painted circa 1503. In 1495 Leonardo began one of his most famous works, the fresco of *The Last Supper*. This became badly damaged over time due to Leonardo's experimentations with the fresco medium, but as recently as 1999 the fresco was finally and controversially restored to its near former glory.

After the fall of Sforza, Leonardo left Milan for brief

spells in Mantua and Venice before returning to Florence in 1500. While here, he engaged in mathematical study and anatomical theory at the hospital of Santa Maria Nuova. In 1502, Leonardo entered the service of Cesare Borgia as a military engineer, and it was at this time that he met and became close friends with Machiavelli, the Italian author and statesman. In 1503 or thereabouts, Leonardo undertook the painting of the celebrated and perhaps his most famous piece, the *Mona Lisa*, which now hangs in the Paris Louvre.

Returning to Milan in 1506, Leonardo was engaged by Charles d'Amboise, in the name of Louis XII, King of France, as an architect and engineer. At this point, Leonardo took a great interest in botany, mechanics, hydraulics, and geology. Leonardo had a large number of pupils at this time and was highly active as a painter and sculptor, painting *St Anne, Mary, and the Child*, which now hangs in the Louvre.

In 1513, Leonardo traveled to Rome, under the patronage of the newly elected Medici Pope, Leo X. By this time, Leonardo was an aging man of 61 and found himself sharing the limelight with Michelangelo and Raphael, the two new young masters who now dominated the artistic arena. While in Rome, Leonardo undertook various engineering and architectural projects at the Vatican as well as receiving several painting commissions. It was from this period that the wonderfully enigmatic *St John the Baptist*, which hangs in the Louvre, was painted.

In 1515, Giuliano de' Medici, the Pope's brother, left Rome, and it is conjectured that Leonardo left Rome with him at this time. Accepting an invitation from Francis I of France, Leonardo settled into his final years at the castle of Cloux, near Amboise, where he continued his great interest in philosophy and science until his death in 1519.

As well as his many other accomplishments, according to the Dossiers Secrets, Leonardo was also one of the Grand

Masters of the Priory of Sion. His undoubted use of symbolism within his paintings and greater work is an area that needs much more research and attention. Leonardo, it is claimed by some researchers, had a major interest in alchemy, especially the alchemical idea of a fusion between male and female being the perfect state. This may well account for his use of androgynous figures within many of his paintings, a good example of this being the painting of John the Baptist, in which the figure of John is strangely hermaphroditic in nature.

In 1965, two previously lost notebooks by Leonardo were found in the National Library of Spain, Madrid. These notebooks contained both a diary and a vast work on technological principles and were published in 1974 as *The Madrid Codices*.

See also: Grand Masters of the Priory of Sion; Last Supper, The; Madonna of the Rocks; Mona Lisa; Vitruvian Man.

Louvre

In the initial chapters of *The Da Vinci Code*, the Louvre Museum in Paris features prominently as the scene of much of the action. It has been the murder scene of Jacques Saunière, the meeting point for Robert Langdon and Sophie Neveu, and, due to the suspicions of Bezu Fache, the starting point of the pursuit that leads eventually to London and on to Scotland.

Although now the home of some of the world's finest pieces of art, the Louvre began its existence as a fortress, built to defend the western approach to Paris. King Philippe

Auguste, who reigned from 1180 to 1223, had towers erected at each corner of the fortress, which lay outside the city ramparts. The royal palace at this time was on Ile de la Cité, and it is hard now to imagine that the site of the Louvre was once outside the boundary of the city. Of this original structure, begun around 1190, only the foundations remain, which were discovered in 1985 during renovations to the Cour Carrée.

Over time, the building was expanded, particularly by Charles V, who added two new wings and had many artists modernizing the Louvre. The city walls of Paris had moved outward and now lay beyond the Louvre, so that it lost its military significance and was used as a royal residence, prison, and arsenal. In 1415, the English, who occupied large parts of France, pillaged the Louvre, and the original treasures were dispersed. The building deteriorated and was neglected, until Francis I in 1528 ordered the demolition of the remaining structure.

In 1546, work began under the supervision of Pierre Lescot of a replacement palace, designed to reflect the wealth and culture of the court, which had a royal art collection that was enlarged by the acquisition of the *Mona Lisa*. After the death of Francis I, his son, Henry II, enthusiastically continued the work, and subsequent monarchs added their own contributions.

A palace built at the nearby Tuileries by Catherine de Médicis was linked to the Louvre by the Grand Gallery, completed in 1606 under Henry IV. The collection of art was continued by Cardinal Richelieu, while work on the buildings continued under Louis XIII and Louis XIV. However, Paris was losing its attraction as a royal residence, and in 1678 the court relocated to Versailles and the Louvre lost its position at the center of political life.

Only members of the court enjoyed the extensive

collection of art and other objects, which numbered around 2,500 in 1715 when Louis XIV died. Some items were put on display in the Luxembourg Palace in 1750, but it took the upheaval of the French Revolution to mark the next phase of the history of the Louvre.

In 1793, the Louvre became a public museum and the Grand Gallery was opened for the public to enjoy the art collection. Napoleon Bonaparte added to the collection during his campaign of conquest in Europe, although many items were returned after his defeat at Waterloo. One of his successors, Napoleon III, who made many changes to the architecture of Paris, also put his stamp on the Louvre with the construction of the Richelieu wing between 1852 and 1857.

The museum today houses paintings by Leonardo Da Vinci, Rembrandt, Titian, and Rubens as well as sculptures such as the *Venus de Milo*. There is a collection of Roman and Greek antiquities, and an Egyptian department that was created in 1826 under the direction of Jean-François Champollion in the same decade as the decipherment of hieroglyphs. By the time of his death in 1832, the department had 9,000 objects, and by acquisition and bequest the collections continued to grow.

In the twentieth century, President Mitterrand embarked on an ambitious project to expand the museum, create modern facilities, and enhance the public spaces. Phase I of the Grand Louvre, which was completed in 1989, includes the famous glass pyramid entrance and an underground space for public amenities. Completed in 1993, Phase II involved the removal of the Ministry of Finance from the Richelieu wing and the wing's conversion to display space. The Carrousel du Louvre was created, an underground complex of shops and facilities, illuminated by the Pyramide Inversée, a glass structure that acts as a skylight. It is this structure that features in the climax of *The Da Vinci Code*. On the anniversary of 200 years as a public museum, the Louvre emerged as a modern structure designed to show off the wonderful objects in its collection of over 300,000 pieces.

See also: Leonardo Da Vinci; Pyramide Inversée; Saunière, Jacques.

Madonna of the Rocks

"So dark the con of man" is an enigmatic clue left on the *Mona Lisa* for Sophie Neveu by her grandfather, Jacques Saunière. It is an anagram, which, when solved, leads her to the picture *Madonna of the Rocks*. Behind the painting she discovers a key that later turns out to be for a safe-deposit box, an important legacy left for her to collect.

Madonna of the Rocks is the name given to two versions of a religious painting by Leonardo Da Vinci that portrays the Virgin Mary sitting with the infant Jesus and John the Baptist, accompanied by an angel, believed to be Archangel Uriel. The composition is triangular in shape, with the Virgin Mary at its apex.

The earlier and more perplexing of the two versions was commissioned on April 25, 1483, for the church of San Francesco Grande in Milan. It is painted with oil on an arched panel, 78 by 48 inches, designed to form the centerpiece of a wooden altar panel within the Chapel of the Immaculate Conception. This center panel was commissioned to depict the Christian legend that describes the Holy Family sheltering in a desert cave in Egypt while fleeing from Herod, and their meeting there with the infant John the Baptist and Uriel, the archangel charged with his protection. Although not mentioned in the Bible, this scene is part of orthodox Christian legend.

The painting features a rocky grotto with a seated Virgin Mary in the center. Beside her sit two infants—Jesus and John the Baptist—while Uriel kneels to her left, slightly behind one of the infants. The child on the Virgin Mary's right, thought to be John the Baptist, kneels beside her, his hands clasped together as in prayer, while the Virgin Mary's right hand embraces his shoulder. To her other side, the infant believed to be Jesus sits cross-legged and slightly away from her, His right hand raised in a gesture of blessing aimed at the other child. Above this, the Virgin Mary's downcast hand hovers over His head and above the pointing finger of Archangel Uriel, who sits behind Him yet is pointing at the other infant sitting on the Virgin's right-hand side.

As neither of the two holy infants were labeled by Leonardo Da Vinci, it is difficult to decide which infant is Jesus and which is John the Baptist. It is, however, generally assumed that the infant administering the blessing is Jesus, with John the Baptist in the more subservient role. This view is encouraged by the second version of the painting, where the child on Mary's right-hand side holds the long reed cross associated with John the Baptist. However, this cross appears to have been added at a later date by another painter and may not have been the intent of Leonardo Da Vinci.

Looking at the painting objectively, it would be more probable that the child praying is Jesus, and not John the Baptist, as this child sits closer to the Virgin Mary and indeed is being cuddled and protected by her. It would then make sense for the other child, who sits farther away from the Virgin, to be John the Baptist, as he then comes under the protection of the archangel with whom he is associated. This is the theory put forward by the authors Clive Prince and Lynn Picknett in their book *The Templar Revelation*—one of the books found on Leigh Teabing's bookshelf by Sophie.

Not surprisingly, many dislike this hypothesis, as it presents John the Baptist in a more important role. This version may, however, hold a deeper symbolism than is readily apparent. For example, the actions of the two infants may reflect the Templar tradition of venerating John the Baptist over Jesus. The pointing action of Uriel is also curious, as is the position of the Virgin Mary's left hand. It has been suggested by Prince and Picknett that Mary's hand is positioned as if clasping an invisible head, while Uriel's pointing finger cuts across the point where an invisible neck would be located. This suggests that Leonardo Da Vinci was effectively labeling the infant below as John the Baptist, who was later beheaded, according to the Bible.

It seems that the co-fraternity who commissioned the painting objected to the lack of Christian references contained in it—there is no depiction of Joseph, for example. As a result it was given to King Louis XII of France and is now in the Louvre. The second version, an oil painting on wood 75 by 47 inches, commissioned in 1503 to replace the earlier one, is now in the National Gallery, London. In this version the figures are slightly larger and have been given halos. Archangel Uriel no longer points toward the infant on the Virgin Mary's right-hand side, who now holds the cross of John the Baptist, as discussed earlier. It would, therefore, appear that all traces of symbolism were removed or expunged in order to meet the requirements of the Church elders.

As Leonardo was allegedly one of the Grand Masters of the Priory of Sion, it is natural for us to look for deeper meanings in his paintings. Certainly, if Leonardo was indeed encoding secret symbolism into his work, the first depiction of the *Madonna of the Rocks* is a prime candidate for this hypothesis.

See also: Leonardo Da Vinci; Neveu, Sophie; Saunière, Jacques.

Mary Magdalene

Intertwined with the central theme of the identity of the Holy Grail, the role of Mary Magdalene is paramount to *The Da Vinci Code*. Brown takes his lead about Mary Magdalene from the book *Holy Blood, Holy Grail*, discussed elsewhere. In this book, the theory is put forward that Mary Magdalene was the wife of Christ and the bearer of His offspring: namely, a female child called Sarah, who perpetuates a whole dynasty of the line of David. This dynasty goes on to become the Merovingian line of kings of France, eventually being driven underground and protected by a secret society known as the Priory of Sion.

This is the theory, but what facts do we know about the Mary Magdalene who appears in the New Testament?

The appellation "Magdalene" is thought to come from the fact that Mary was from the town of Magdala. She appears surprisingly few times in the New Testament, and her appearances can be categorized as four distinct types: with a traveling entourage, at the Crucifixion, at the burial of Christ, and witnessing the Resurrection.

One thing we can say for certain: the long-held belief that Mary Magdalene was a repentant prostitute is a false one. The idea that Mary was in fact a prostitute seems to be a mistake. In the sixth century, Pope Gregory I issued a proclamation that Mary Magdalene was a sinful woman, a repentant prostitute, but he seemed to be amalgamating three different women, as well as misunderstanding Luke 7 and 8. This situation, of course, wasn't helped by the Church, which until 1969, when the Vatican issued a quiet retraction, still held that Mary was a fallen woman.

From the Gospels, it can be seen that Mary plays very much the part of one of the disciples. She is with Jesus at three of His key moments: looking on as He is crucified, helping with His burial, and being the first person to encounter the resurrected Christ. These facts in themselves mark her out as, at the very least, symbolically important and may account for Peter being so disparaging of her, as we shall see.

Is there any evidence for a closer relationship between the Magdalene and Jesus? The New Testament sadly fails us in this respect. A straight reading of the Gospels gives us no insight into any potential relationship between the two: indeed, its silence on the matter is deafening. Having stated this, however, it should be remembered that the New Testament, as we have it today, has gone through many stages of editing and additions to the text. It has also been through many translations to get to where we have it now. So what about sources outside the traditional Gospels?

One of the so-called Church Fathers, Hippolytus, in his commentary on the Song of Songs, does seem to mention Mary, albeit in a roundabout way:

> Lest the female Apostles doubt the angels, Christ himself came to them so that the women be Apostles of Christ and by their obedience rectify the sin of ancient Eve.

He goes on to say how Christ had shown Himself to the male Apostles and says: "It is I who appeared to these women and I who wanted to send them to you as Apostles."

In the Gospel of Philip (63: 33–6), one of the so-called Gnostic Gospels found with the Nag Hammadi hoard in Egypt, more obscure language is used to describe a possible close relationship between Jesus and Mary Magdalene. In this text, it is stated that Jesus used to "love her more than all the disciples" and that He used to "kiss her often on the mouth," the male disciples being particularly offended by this behavior. Although there is no hint of actual marriage or cohabitation here, the word used to describe Mary in the Coptic language of the texts is *koinonos*, which has been translated by Susan

Haskins (in her 1993 book *Mary Magdalene: Myth and Metaphor*) as meaning "consort" or "partner."

One of the Nag Hammadi texts is known as the Gospel of Mary. In it we find a reference to the fact that she was the recipient of revelation, much to the annoyance of the male Apostles. In 17: 10–18 of the Gospel, we find Andrew doubting that Mary had actually seen the resurrected Christ and Peter asking: "Did He really speak with a woman without our knowledge and not openly?" He goes on to say: "Did He prefer her to us?" Later in the text, Levi goes on to castigate Peter, saying: "But if the Savior made her worthy, who are you indeed to reject her? Surely the Savior knows her very well. That is why He loved her more than us."

What these texts do show us is that the role of the women followers of Jesus may well have been of a higher status than we are led to believe, but they don't shed any light on the central question of whether Mary and Jesus were man and wife. Rather, they give us tantalizing glimpses and possibilities and allow trains of thought and theories to be based on supposition. We have to remember that the above quoted texts are just a few out of the hundreds of texts that relate to this period.

One thought-provoking theory put forward by the authors of *Holy Blood, Holy Grail* is that the story in the Bible of the Wedding at Cana, where Jesus performs the miracle of turning water into wine, may actually be a distorted telling of Jesus' own wedding. This theory has much to recommend it and may well be one of the major clues needed to settle this argument. This, and the fact that Jesus, as a Jew at that time, would have been expected to marry, are intriguing possibilities.

What we are left with are these conclusions:

• The character of Mary Magdalene in the New Testament may well have had a closer relationship to Jesus than was originally thought.

• Mary was with Jesus at key stages of the story, notably the death, burial, and Resurrection of Christ.

• There is no direct evidence within the currently known texts and Gospels that corroborates the idea that Jesus and Mary were married.

• Even the Gospels found at Nag Hammadi (in 1945) are silent in their evidence (or lack thereof) in this matter, apart from a reference in Philip to a possible consort.

What happened to Mary after the death of Christ? According to Catholic tradition, Mary Magdalene died in Ephesus, where she had resided along with Mary, Mother of Jesus, and John, the supposed author of the fourth Gospel. This tradition is disputed, though, by a sixth-century legend mentioned by Gregory of Tours, which states that an even earlier document offers the story that Mary Magdalene traveled to Aix-en-Provence, in France, in the entourage of St Maximin. It is this story that seems to be the catalyst for the Sang Raal (blood royal, or royal bloodline of Christ) theories of modern times. Mary Magdalene is also known as the "beloved" in Gnostic circles, so linking her again with the idea of a union with Jesus. For more on the ideas behind this, it is worth reading *The Woman with the Alabaster Jar* by Margaret Starbird. The same author also claims, in her 1993 book *The Goddess in the Gospels: Reclaiming the Sacred Feminine*, that under the ancient Hebrew system of *gematria*, or number symbolism, the name Mary Magdalene and its number of 153 in this system indicate that Mary was the "goddess" in this context. Starbird also believes that Mary spent much time in the flourishing cosmopolitan and burgeoning Gnostic city of Alexandria. Again, this could account for much of the myths and legends that surround this character, as can be seen in the numerous cults of the Magdalene that grew up around the Mediterranean in the first few centuries AD.

It would seem that the theory of a lineage from Christ is not a new one in itself, but the theory that it was Mary Magdalene who bore Him a child seems to be very modern indeed (see the entry on *Holy Blood, Holy Grail* for more on this). A whole industry has also grown up in modern times around the Magdalene as an embodiment of the Sacred Feminine, who somehow represents the spirit of the Mother Goddess. This is a wholly different approach to the bloodline theory, insomuch that it is based more on metaphor and symbolism than on actual physical reality. It would seem logical that the role of Mary Magdalene is either as the consort of Jesus or as a personification of the Sacred Feminine.

The story of Mary Magdalene is wrapped up in myth, legend, and symbolism. She has come to represent and stand for the very spirit of the ancient goddess that was worshipped throughout the Middle East and Europe millennia ago. Whether she was indeed married to Jesus, or bore Him a child, is quite simply not provable as history stands today. These stories remain shrouded in myth but are destined to become louder as we move through time. Two thousand years of the repression of the feminine will see to that.

See also: Gnostics; Goddess Worship; Holy Blood, Holy Grail.

Merovingians

In *The Da Vinci Code*, Sophie Neveu discovers that her family has been connected with an organization, the Priory of Sion, which believes in a bloodline descended from Jesus and Mary Magdalene. She is told that this supposed bloodline was passed through the Merovingian kings of France, and this connects with a story she remembers from school about King Dagobert being stabbed in the eye.

The Merovingians were the ruling family in a kingdom spanning parts of modern France and Germany from around AD 447 to 750. The dynasty took its name from Merovech (Latinized as Meroveus), who was a chief of the Franks, one of a group of Germanic tribes that had entered the Roman Empire and started to establish their rule.

In 481, Clovis I succeeded to the Merovingian throne, becoming the first king of that line, and he extended his realm by defeating the last Roman official in northern Gaul and capturing most of the area north of the River Loire. He also defeated the Visigoths and added most of Aquitaine to his dominions. Clovis married a Burgundian princess called Clotilde who was a Roman Catholic, a religion to which he converted, possibly under her influence and that of her confessor, St Remy. Interestingly, Remy is the name of Leigh Teabing's servant in *The Da Vinci Code*.

The conversion to Catholicism was a major step, as the Franks, along with other tribes such as the Goths and Visigoths, held Arian beliefs. This principle, named for Arius, a fourth-century priest from Alexandria, Egypt, was that although Jesus was the Son of God, Jesus and God were two separate beings. Since Jesus had been created, rather than being co-eternal with God the Father and the Holy Spirit, Arians denied the existence of the Trinity. The Arian "heresy" had been condemned at the Council of Nicaea, and the Roman Emperor Constantine tried to have Arian documents destroyed.

Clovis I is also renowned for having made Paris the capital of his extended kingdom, thus ensuring him a place in French history. After the death of Clovis, the kingdom was divided between his four sons, and for the next 150 years the Merovingian dynasty was ruled either centrally or by branches of the family in different regional centers. During this time, the kings came to rely more and more on officials, whose title was Mayor of the Palace.

Dagobert II acceded in 676, and it was this king who is the unfortunate monarch believed to have been stabbed to death through the eye, on the orders of Pepin the Fat, his Mayor of the Palace. From his second marriage to a Visigoth princess, Dagobert had a son, Sigisbert, who, according to the authors of *Holy Blood, Holy Grail*, escaped and thus continued the bloodline.

The last of the Merovingian monarchs, Childeric III, was deposed in 751 and sent to a monastery after his long hair had been cut. The significance of the Merovingian kings having long hair is not understood, but they were known by their contemporaries as the "long-haired kings."

See also: Constantine the Great; Council of Nicaea; Holy Blood, Holy Grail.

Mithras

In order to understand the controversy surrounding the Council of Nicaea and the origins of the modern Christian Church, Sophie Neveu learns about the links to the pre-Christian god Mithras.

Originally an ancient god of Persia and India, where he

was known as Mitra, Mithras was a minor god within the Zoroastrian system until around the sixth century BC. It wasn't until the rise of the Achaemenid dynasty in Persia that this god became increasingly important, when in the fifth century BC he reappeared as the principal god of the Persians, a god of light and wisdom and very closely associated with the sun.

Expanding throughout the Middle East and southern Europe, the cult of Mithraism was soon established as a major religion and became one of the great religions of the Roman Empire. In the second century AD, Mithraism was a bigger religious movement than the fledgling Christian sect. Mithras, as the god was known in Latin, was the god par excellence for the Roman legionaries, being a great comrade and fighter in the eyes of the cult followers, with the fundamental and central aspect of the Mithraic system being the dualistic struggle between the forces of light and darkness, good and evil.

Central to the Mithras story is how Mithras captures and sacrifices a sacred bull, from whose sacrificed body springs all the beneficent things of the earth. The cult was similar in many ways to some of the mystery cults that sprang up in those formative years, with baptism and sacramental forms that closely resembled many other cults and with interwoven similarities to Christianity also present: for instance, the Feast Day of the birth of Mithras being celebrated on December 25.

See also: Council of Nicaea.

Mona Lisa

The most famous painting in the world, Leonardo's *Mona Lisa* hangs in the Louvre in Paris and is featured in *The Da Vinci Code* when it is to this painting that Sophie and Langdon are guided in their search for another of Jacques Saunière's clues scrawled on the Plexiglas protecting the painting.

Probably painted between 1503 and 1506, with a little addition in 1510, the *Mona Lisa* is undoubtedly one of the most famous faces in the world. Yet we are not absolutely sure who the sitter was. The painting was executed for a Florentine silk merchant called Francesco del Giocondo, and most art historians assume that the painting is an image of Lisa Gherardini, the wife of Giocondo, who commissioned the portrait as a celebration to mark the birth of their second son in December of 1502. However, debates have raged for the best part of 500 years as to whether it is actually her.

The word Mona is actually a contraction of Monna, which in turn is a contraction of Madonna, or Mia Donna, meaning "My Lady" or "Madam." It would seem that the English rendition of Mona Lisa is due to a spelling error at some time in the past. In French the painting is known as *La Joconde* and in Italian *La Gioconda*, meaning "the merry one" but also a play on the name of the assumed sitter.

The painting shows a brilliant use of a technique known as sfumato, which is a type of blurring and blending of the paint that fuses one tone into another. In the *Mona Lisa*, Leonardo shows what a master of this technique he had become, defining the corners of the eyes and mouth with such precision and beauty that the painting has an almost dreamlike quality.

One anomaly on the painting is that the figure has no eyebrows. This could be a result of over-zealous cleaning of the masterpiece at some time in the past or simply the sitter completely plucking out her eyebrows, as was then the fashion.

Some alternative researchers have claimed that the painting is actually a self-portrait of Leonardo, being defined as a female, or even in hermaphroditic form. Indeed, if you were to remove the hair of the figure, you would be left with a strangely asexual set of facial features. This theory was strengthened when two independent researchers, Lillian Schwartz of Bell Labs and Dr Digby Quested of the Maudsley Hospital in London, both demonstrated that the *Mona Lisa* could in fact be interpreted as a self-portrait of Leonardo, by taking the later famous self-portrait of him as an old man and "morphing" the features onto the *Mona Lisa* using modern computer techniques. The results were startling. It would seem that the female *Mona Lisa* is a very close mirror image of the master's face, with all the major facial lines matching, including the tip of the nose, lips, and eyes.

In 1911, the *Mona Lisa* was stolen by Vincenzo Peruggia, an Italian woodworker employed at the Louvre. Peruggia simply walked out of the Salon Carré in the Louvre, where the painting used to hang, with the masterpiece hidden under his workman's smock. It wasn't recovered until 1913, when he attempted to sell the work to a collector. He had kept the most famous painting in the world in the false bottom of a trunk. It seems that Peruggia believed a large number of Italian works of art in the Louvre had been stolen by Napoleon and he wanted to return the *Mona Lisa* to its rightful Italian home.

See also: Leonardo Da Vinci; Louvre.

Neveu, Sophie

Sophie is one of the leading characters in *The Da Vinci Code*, and the actions of her grandfather, Jacques Saunière, set her on a quest of discovery that will change her life.

Her name is important, as Sofia, which appears in the New Testament meaning "wisdom," is the solution to one of the puzzles she has to solve. Sophie has been brought up in Paris by Saunière, who nicknamed her Princess Sophie. This conveniently hid the initials P.S., which also represent the Priory of Sion, the organization of which he is the Grand Master. The Priory believes that a bloodline descends from Jesus, through His marriage to Mary Magdalene. It is interesting, therefore, that in French Sophie's surname, Neveu, means "descendant." The knowledge that she gains about her family as the book progresses, and the understanding of the Priory's activities, seem to have been foretold in her name.

See also: Mary Magdalene; Priory of Sion; Saunière, Jacques.

Newton, Sir Isaac

In London, Robert Langdon and Sophie Neveu find themselves searching for the clues to unlock a cryptex. They are led to the tomb in Westminster Abbey of Sir Isaac Newton, the first scientist to be knighted.

Isaac Newton was born at Woolsthorpe, England, on December 25, 1642, using the Julian calendar (or January 4, 1643, using the Gregorian). His father had already died before his birth, so Isaac was brought up for his first three years solely by his mother. When Hannah Newton married Barnabas Smith in 1646, she left home, and Isaac entered the care of his grandparents. This arrangement lasted until Hannah was again widowed after around eight years of marriage, and she returned with the three children from this marriage, Isaac's half siblings.

Soon after his mother's return, Isaac, at the age of 12, was once again separated from her when he attended King's School in Grantham, Lincolnshire. The school was too far from home for him to travel daily, and so he lodged with the family of a local apothecary, or herbalist, a Mr Clark. Newton's notebooks from this period show that he used to take a keen interest in the work of the apothecary, which began a lifelong interest in remedies and cures.

The school's headmaster, Henry Stokes, clearly saw Newton's potential, despite the fact that his pupil was not initially outstanding, and he must have been frustrated when Hannah withdrew her son from school at the age of 16. Isaac returned home, but he was not suited to life on the farm. After influence from Stokes and Hannah's brother, William Ayscough, himself educated at Cambridge, it was agreed that Isaac would return to school to prepare for university at Trinity College, Cambridge.

In 1661, Newton began a long affinity with Cambridge University, initially on a very lowly basis. He was a subsizar, later a sizar, which meant that he had to work to pay his expenses and to support himself during his studies. It seems that although she was a wealthy widow, Newton's mother was not inclined to make it easy for her son to indulge his academic interests. Despite this disadvantage, Newton took his Bachelor's degree in 1665, and he then returned to his family home in Woolsthorpe, where he spent most of the next 18 months.

The reason for this extended absence from the university was the outbreak of plague that claimed many lives. Despite not being at Trinity College, Newton worked on mathematical concepts, and the two years 1665 and 1666 are referred to as Newton's *anni mirabiles*.

A process to calculate the summation of the arcs of a curve, the technique involved in calculus, provided a platform to study the movements of planets in orbit. His study of the forces applied to planets was to lead to his theory of gravity.

The plague, which had caused people to disperse, was receding, and the university reopened in 1667. Newton was nominated as a Fellow of Trinity College, and he also acquired his Master's degree. He was now entitled to a job for life at the university, and when in 1669 the position of Lucasian Professor of Mathematics was confirmed, Newton had achieved a rapid ascent of the academic ladder.

The Anglican Church was a central pillar of public and academic life to which Newton officially needed to subscribe. His own beliefs were Puritan, and he focused his energies on his studies, ignoring temptations that might distract him. In 1674, it took the intervention of a friend who was the king's chaplain to exempt him from having to take holy orders.

One of the main interests of Newton was the behavior of light, and he proposed that white light was made up of a band of colors and not a single entity, a belief held since Aristotle's day. He experimented with prisms and presented the Royal Society with his invention, the reflecting telescope, being elected a Fellow of the Society in 1672.

Newton was able to build on his understanding of the laws of motion and the effect of a centrifugal force applied to an object moving in a circular path. He derived the inverse square law, and using his calculus he showed that planets were attracted to the sun by this force. In his book *The*

Mathematical Principles of Natural Philosophy (*Philosophiae Naturalis Principia Mathematica*), known as the *Principia*, he managed to explain variations in the moon's orbit, the action of tides, and the precession of the earth's axis. This work was published in 1687 and has been seen as the greatest scientific book ever written.

For a man who developed many of the scientific principles in use today, Newton had a very unorthodox interest: alchemy, the mystical art of transforming base metals into gold. It occupied a great proportion of his time, and he left notebooks filled with his work, although he never published any of his alchemical studies.

The basis of the belief in alchemy was derived from Aristotle's description of the four elements, combined with the notion that under the right conditions one material may be converted into another if the proportion of their component elements is adjusted. As the Arabs refined the practice from the fourth century, metals were regarded as compounds of sulfur and mercury. It followed that one metal—lead, say—could be converted into another—such as gold—by altering the balance of sulfur and mercury. The *Corpus Hermeticum*, a manuscript from the second or third century purported to have been written by Hermes Trismegistus, kindled interest in alchemy in Europe.

Newton's first experiments were an attempt to produce the philosopher's stone, which alchemists believed was the catalyst that would convert metals, as described above. He produced a form of antimony called the star regulus and described in a letter of 1672 that one of the uses for this product was making a mirror for a telescope. This shows the links that appear between Newton's orthodox discoveries in the field of light, gravity, and mathematics and the discipline that kept him occupied in his rooms at Cambridge.

After 35 years at Cambridge, in 1696 Isaac Newton left for

London to take up a post as Warden of the Mint, an administrative position with the government-controlled supplier of coin. This change did not prevent his scientific career from continuing, and he was elected President of the Royal Society in 1703. Another major publication, *Opticks*, appeared in 1704, and it was shortly after this that Queen Anne bestowed a knighthood on him.

When he died in 1727, Sir Isaac Newton was buried in Westminster Abbey after a state funeral. The pallbearers were the Lord Chancellor, two dukes, and three earls, and a monument was erected to this extraordinary man.

The papers Newton wrote of his studies in alchemy were bought in 1936 by the economist John Maynard Keynes, who, during a speech to mark 300 years of the anniversary of Newton's birth, explained: "He regarded the universe as a cryptogram set by the Almighty."

See also: Newton's Monument; Pope, Alexander.

Newton's Monument

Completed in 1731, the monument to the great scientist Sir Isaac Newton, erected in Westminster Abbey, was designed by William Kent and the sculpture executed by Michael Rysbrack. Robert and Sophie solve a puzzle to find this location, at which they believe they will find another clue; however, Teabing has beaten them to the site.

Newton reclines on the sarcophagus with his elbow resting on some of his greatest works: "Divinity," "Chronology," "Opticks," and "Philo. Prin. Math." The last book is the renowned masterpiece *Philosophiae Naturalis Principia Mathematica*, often known as the *Principia*. Two winged boys hold a scroll with a mathematical design on it, and in the background is a pyramid with a celestial globe with the zodiac signs on it. A panel on the sarcophagus depicts the instruments used by Newton in his work, including a telescope and a prism.

The inscription, which is in Latin, translates as:

Here is buried Isaac Newton, Knight, who by strength of mind almost divine, and mathematical principles peculiarly his own, explored the course and figures of the planets, the paths of comets, the tides of the sea, the dissimilarities in rays of light, and, what no other scholar has previously imagined, the properties of the colors thus produced. Diligent, sagacious, and faithful in his expositions of nature, antiquity, and the Holy Scriptures, he vindicated by his philosophy the majesty of God mighty and good, and expressed the simplicity of the Gospel in his manners. Mortals rejoice that there has existed such and so great an ornament of the human race! He was born on December 25, 1642, and died on March 20, 1726.

See also: Newton, Sir Isaac.

Opus Dei

This is the organization to which two characters in *The Da Vinci Code* belong: namely, Manuel Aringarosa and Silas.

Founded by Josemaria Escriva de Balaguer in Spain on October 2, 1928, this Catholic organization's stated aim is to "spread throughout society a profound awareness of the universal call to holiness and apostolate through one's professional work carried out with freedom and personal responsibility" (quoted from *Encyclopedia of Associations*). Made up of lay members and priests, Opus Dei has been at the center of controversy many times in its existence. Its lay members work in the secular world, but always under strict spiritual direction, following what is known as the "plan of life": daily spiritual practices, readings, and mental prayers, as well as specific Opus Dei customs and in some cases corporal mortification.

Opus Dei is Latin for "work of God" or "God's work." The organization boasts over 80,000 members in some 60 countries worldwide. The headquarters is in Rome, and in 1982 Pope John Paul II elected the organization as a personal prelature, conveying great status and implying his support. Its founder, Josemaria Escriva, was canonized by the same Pope on October 6, 2002. Escriva wrote a book, called *The Way*, in which he states: "Blessed be pain. Loved be pain. Sanctified be pain... Glorified be pain." Statements like these reinforce the idea that the organization practices

severe corporal mortification. It has been said that Escriva used to whip his own back so harshly that his room walls would be splattered with blood.

The Catholicism as practiced by Opus Dei members, while not doctrinally divergent from what could be classed as "standard" Catholicism, is certainly a much stricter reading of the Scriptures and Gospels in relation to how some of the members lead their lives.

The membership classes of Opus Dei are very particular in their makeup:

Numerary: These are the members who generally live in Opus Dei houses and lead a life of celibacy. The sexes are strictly segregated, and the members dedicate a good deal, if not all, of their salaries to Opus Dei. Corporal mortification is also claimed to be carried out by these members (see also Cilice Belt). In the book, Silas is meant to have been a Numerary of Opus Dei.

Supernumerary: These lesser Numeraries generally live within the community at large; some marry and have children, but all still follow the same "plan of life" as set down for the Numeraries. A good portion of a Supernumerary's income is also dedicated to Opus Dei.

Numerary Priests: These are generally lay members of the order who have been handpicked by the Opus Dei hierarchy to become priests. Many Numerary Priests go on to hold top positions within the Opus Dei network, some even within the Vatican itself.

Associate Members: Many Associate Members also commit to a life of celibacy, but they do not live within Opus Dei houses.

Numerary Assistants: These are generally women who are responsible for the upkeep, care, and cleaning of the Opus Dei houses. Most lead a celibate life.

Cooperators: While not considered members, Cooperators are supporters of Opus Dei who pledge money and any other support they can to the cause. These are the only class who do not have to be of the Catholic faith.

As is mentioned in *The Da Vinci Code*, Opus Dei does indeed have a shiny new headquarters in New York City, at 243 Lexington Avenue, the 17-story building having no sign to announce its occupants. Inside the building are two chapels, a library, conference rooms, living quarters, and dining rooms. The Vatican yearbook counts some 3,000 members in the USA, with around 60 Opus Dei residences scattered throughout the American mainland. As an organization, Opus Dei has attracted a great deal of attention because of its obvious wealth. Many rich individuals and families are Cooperators of Opus Dei, meaning that they donate large sums to the organization. Many of these are not of the Catholic doctrine, but see in Opus Dei an organization ready to defend the Church and greater Christianity against all who would oppose it.

See also: Aringarosa, Manuel; Cilice Belt; Silas.

Osiris

Sophie Neveu learns about Osiris when she is being enlightened by Robert Langdon and Leigh Teabing. Langdon and Teabing explain that much of what we consider to be Christian beliefs have actually been absorbed from an earlier Osirian cult. It is this alternative view of Christian history that underpins the novel.

Osiris is the ancient Egyptian god of the underworld (*duat*) and is connected with death, fertility, and resurrection. His name is written in hieroglyphs as a throne and an eye and is translated as *wsr*, meaning "Mighty One." Other epithets for Osiris include Wennefer ("Eternally Good"), Khentimentiu ("Foremost of the Westerners," i.e. the deceased, emphasizing the funerary role of Osiris), "He who dwells in Orion with a season in the sky and a season on earth," indicating his association with the constellation Orion and the deceased king's transformation as a stellar god.

Pictorially, Osiris is shown as an erect or seated mummy, his hands protruding from the mummy wrappings in order to hold the crook and flail of kingship. On his unwrapped head Osiris wears the *atef* crown, a tall, conical white crown with a plume on either side, sometimes also sporting ram's horns on the front of the crown.

As with most Egyptian gods, Osiris's origins are vague, but it would appear that he was one of the earliest gods and was originally a fertility god associated with grain and the harvest. As the cult of Osiris "the Old One" grew and spread to other centers in Egypt, Osiris gradually took on the attributes of the local gods he overtook. Thus, Osiris took over the insignia and regalia of Andjety from Busaris, and some of the attributes of Khentimentiu, the ancient jackal-god of Abydos, as well as of Sokar. Osiris, therefore, acquired the characteristics of a protective funerary god.

The Pyramid Texts, the oldest written corpus of Egyptian

religious, funerary, and magical literature dating to the fourth and fifth dynasties (2492–2181 BC), state that Osiris was born at Rosetau in the Nile Delta to the gods Geb and Nut, being brother to Isis, Seth, Nephthys, and Thoth. From the Old Kingdom (2686–2181 BC), Osiris was closely linked to the pharaoh in that on a king's death he became Osiris, king of the underworld.

The mythology relating to Osiris revolves around his unjust death at the hands of Seth, his brother, the discovery of his body by his sister Isis, and his subsequent resurrection and impregnation of Isis with the aid of her magical knowledge. Earlier myth states that his brother Thoth and son Horus mummified his body, and Osiris henceforth became the god of the underworld.

In later periods the mythology surrounding the death of Osiris was developed further, entailing the dismemberment of Osiris's body by Seth, which he then threw into the Nile. Isis retrieves all the pieces of his body (between 14 and 42, depending on the text) and reassembles them into the form of Osiris as a mummy. Only the phallus could not be found, as it had been eaten by a Nile carp, so an artificial penis was made and Isis used magical spells to conceive a child with this. At each location where a part of Osiris was discovered, a temple was built in his honor, notably Sebennytos, which claimed the upper and lower leg, Herakleopolis the thigh, head, two sides, and two legs, Athribis the heart, Abydos the head, Edfu a leg, and Biga Island the left leg. Because the penis had been eaten by a carp, the Pyramid Texts depict fish by mutilating the signs, so that a fish will be depicted cut in half, or without a tail, fin, or head. This is because the Egyptians thought that every depiction and hieroglyph had a life of its own and that a potentially dangerous animal/object could harm the deceased.

At Abydos a festival of Osiris was an annual enactment of

the Osiris legend and the "mysteries" of the god. The god is heralded in by the canine god Wepwawet, followed by a procession of the shrine of Osiris aboard a boat that is carried to his symbolic tomb. A mock battle then ensues to represent Osiris destroying his enemies (although Herodotus notes that the mock battle often incurred fatalities). The ceremonial boat and shrine are then returned to the temple of Abydos for a number of purification rites.

From the Middle and New Kingdom (2055–1069 BC), Osiris's exclusive association with the deceased king had spread to include all the "blessed dead," and private funerary formulas were addressed to Osiris through the bounty of the king. The underworld realm of Osiris is only for those souls worthy enough to enter and, as such, Osiris sits in judgment of the recently deceased. In the Pyramid Texts he is sometimes referred to as "Lord of Maat," Maat being the goddess of truth.

The *djed* pillar is the symbol of Osiris, and *The Book of the Dead* states that it represents the backbone of the god, indicating stability. Its form is of a pillar that has at least three crossbars near the top. Although associated with Osiris, it does in fact date to a much earlier time and may represent a threshing pole for grain.

Osiris as a deity who is resurrected, and one whose son forms an integral part of his myth, has a direct parallel in the Christian story. For the Egyptian deceased, a judgment awaited presided over by Osiris, where their deeds would be weighed to decide what their eternal fate would be.

See also: Isis; Langdon, Robert; Neveu, Sophie; Teabing, Leigh.

Pentagram

In *The Da Vinci Code*, when Jacques Saunière is found dead in the Louvre, he is laid out in the shape of the Leonardo drawing, the *Vitruvian Man*, which in turn takes the form of a pentagram.

The pentagram is essentially a five-pointed star. Also known as a pentacle, the pentagram has come to represent dark or black magic in the eyes of many Christians, although its origins were actually as a talisman or sacred geometrical sign and can be traced at least as far back as ancient Greece. The word "pentagram" comes from the ancient Greek, meaning "five lines," although the symbol itself was in use far earlier. The Greek word may itself derive from ancient Mesopotamia around 3000 BC, where it is said to mean "heavenly body" or "star." In Egypt, the five-pointed pentagram within the circle was representative of the *duat* or underworld of Egyptian mythology and symbolism.

In Christian tradition, the pentagram was once used to represent the five wounds, or stigmata, of Christ. To the Pythagoreans, the five points represented the five classical elements: fire, earth, air, water, and idea, or divine thing. The Pythagoreans also saw within the pentagram mathematical perfection and realized among other things that the pentagram hides within its lines the Golden Ratio of 1.618. In black magic circles, or Satanic symbolism, the pentagram is reversed, with the point facing down, and in this form it can be said to represent the head of Baphomet, with the two upward points corresponding to a pair of horns. Its use as a Satanic symbol seems to be a fairly modern one, with no real precedent or associated use in ancient times. In Hebrew tradition, the five-pointed pentagram was associated with the five books of the Pentateuch, the first five books of the Old Testament supposedly written by Moses.

The pentagram was also known as the Star of Solomon in

some sources, or Solomon's Seal, and it is used in Arabic magical traditions and rituals as well as Jewish rituals. The first mention of the pentagram in the English language seems to be in the 1380 Arthurian story, *Sir Gawain and the Green Knight*, where Gawain has a shield with the pentagram emblazoned on it.

See also: Baphomet; Golden Ratio; Vitruvian Man.

Plantard, Pierre

Also known as Pierre Plantard de St-Clair. Elected on January 17, 1981, Plantard was the Grand Master of the Priory of Sion and public liaison for the order in the early 1980s when Baigent, Leigh, and Lincoln were researching and writing *Holy Blood, Holy Grail*. In *The Da Vinci Code*, the connection between Sophie Neveu and her family to the Priory of Sion becomes more apparent with time. She is taught about Plantard and discovers from her grandmother at the conclusion of her search that she is a member of both the Plantard and St-Clair families.

The genealogies in the Dossiers Secrets support Plantard's claim that he is a direct descendant of the Merovingian King Dagobert II. Therefore, when Plantard intimated that one of the purposes of the Priory of Sion was to restore the Merovingian dynasty to the French throne, he was actually implying that he himself was the rightful heir. Although traditional historical sources claim that Dagobert II was assassinated in 679 without an heir, Plantard claimed that

Priory records confirm that Dagobert had a son, Sigisbert IV, by a secret second marriage and that the sacred Merovingian bloodline continued unbroken through the centuries to Plantard himself.

Most of the information available today on the Priory of Sion appears to have been masterminded by Pierre Plantard in one form or another, leaked via a variety of self-published newsletters, cryptic manuscripts, or convoluted genealogies that were deposited in the Bibliothèque Nationale in Paris, or sometimes via interviews with trusted spokesmen. The literature generated by the Priory was often characterized by the use of esoteric double meanings and a high degree of in-jokes, which have piqued the curiosity of many a "Grail buff" who has tried to decipher the enigmatic Priory documents over the decades. It seems that Plantard's reasons for leaking much of this information was to seed the idea that he was the rightful heir to the throne of France, rather than to say that the Priory of Sion protected a supposed bloodline of Christ, which he never claimed.

Although a multitude of books had been written about the Priory of Sion in France, both Plantard and the society gained international public recognition only after the publication of *Holy Blood, Holy Grail* in 1982. It appears that this success inevitably caused a degree of infighting within the order, and it also spawned a large number of copycat chivalric orders and secret societies, which made claims of superiority based on their own "secret" documents, family archives, and convoluted genealogies.

As the situation became more complex, Pierre Plantard finally resigned as Grand Master of the Priory of Sion on July 11, 1984, citing his health and disagreements with certain American members of the order, enigmatically referred to as the "American contingent," though who this contingent is remains a mystery.

Plantard died on February 3, 2000. His body was cremated, but the location of his final resting place is unknown.

See also: Dossiers Secrets; Merovingians; Neveu, Sophie; Priory of Sion.

Pope, Alexander

The second cryptex, or puzzle, that Robert Langdon and Sophie need to decode has the clue "In London lies a knight a Pope interred..." After a database search, they realize that the Pope referred to is the British poet and satirist Alexander Pope (1688–1744).

The knight in question is Sir Isaac Newton, of whom Pope wrote the following lines:

> Nature and nature's laws
> Lay hid in night;
> God said, *Let Newton be!*
> And all was light.

Pope was paying tribute to Newton's making possible greater understanding of the movement of planets and of the study of light. Newton had invented a telescope that he presented to the Royal Society in London.

The reference to the knight's interment in the clue leads the characters to Newton's tomb in Westminster Abbey, where he was buried.

Alexander Pope was born in London, the son of a linen merchant. Excluded from mainstream education as a result of his Roman Catholic faith, he was prevented from attending university or holding public office. Despite this, he was proficient in Latin and Greek, later earning the considerable sum of £2,000 for translations of Homer's *Iliad* and *Odyssey* into English. Following a childhood illness, probably a tubercular condition of the spine called Pott's disease, Pope grew to only 4 feet 6 inches in height and had to wear a stiffened bodice throughout his life to support his hunchbacked spine.

Pope's first major work, *An Essay on Criticism*, was published in 1711 when he was only 23 years old. It contained the still-famous quote "a little learning is a dangerous thing." *The Rape of the Lock* was another work that used satire to ridicule the fashionable world of high society.

In his time, Pope was famous for his bitter literary quarrels. *The Dunciad*, written originally in 1728 then amended in 1742, was a scathing satire on critics and bad writers, and in *Imitations of Horace* Pope attacked a former friend, Lady Mary Wortley Montagu.

Despite his reputation for conflict, Alexander Pope had many friends, including Jonathan Swift, Robert Harley (first Earl of Oxford), and Martha Blount, to whom he left his property on his death in 1744. He was also clearly an admirer of Sir Isaac Newton, as shown from his generous tribute.

See also: Newton, Sir Isaac; Newton's Monument.

Priory of Sion

The centuries-old secret society whose invisible existence underpins the entire plot of *The Da Vinci Code*. The murder of Jacques Saunière, Sophie Neveu's grandfather, who is subsequently revealed to be the Grand Master of the Priory of Sion, is the catalyst that triggers Sophie's and Robert Langdon's quest to discover the location of the Priory's grand secret before it falls into the hands of the Priory's arch-nemesis, Opus Dei.

According to the Priory of Sion's "official" history in their archives, the Dossiers Secrets, the Order of Sion was founded in 1090 in the Holy Land by Godfroy de Boullion, who captured Jerusalem in 1099. After Jerusalem fell to the Crusaders, Godfroy ordered the construction of the Abbey of Notre-Dame du Mont de Sion to be built on the ruins of an ancient Byzantine church located outside the walls of Jerusalem, south of the Sion Gate. This abbey housed an order of Augustinian canons who served as advisers to Godfroy and who, Priory documents claim, were secretly involved in the creation of the Knights Templar in 1118, to serve as the Order of Sion's military and exterior administrative arm.

In 1152 a small contingent from the Abbey of Notre-Dame du Mont de Sion accompanied the French King Louis VII back to France after the Second Crusade and were installed at St-Samson in Orléans. A more select offshoot of this group was housed at the "little priory of the Mount of Sion" nearby at St-Jean-le-Blanc on the outskirts of Orléans. According to Priory documents, this was the inception of the secret order that came to be known as the Priory of Sion.

The Priory of Sion and the Knights Templar operated concurrently until a major dispute resulted in an official split between the two orders at Gisors in Normandy in 1188, known as the Cutting of the Elm. The Dossiers Secrets state that, after relations between the two orders were cut, the Knights Templar continued to function publicly, growing in importance with their own independent Grand Masters until their eventual dissolution in 1307. However, the Priory of Sion is said to have gone underground at this point, adopting the alternative name of the Order of the Rose-Cross Veritas, also codenamed Ormus, after the French word "orme," meaning "elm." By implication, this was the origin of the esoteric movement that later surfaced in European history as Rosicrucianism.

The Grand Masters of the underground Priory of Sion have traditionally been known as "Nautonniers," or "Navigators." The first official Navigator of the Priory of Sion was Jean de Gisors, who was present at the Cutting of the Elm at Gisors and served from 1188 until his death in 1220 under the title of Jean II. The Navigators of the Priory of Sion appear to have passed the leadership down through a specific family bloodline, but later this position passes through some of the most influential artists, scientists, and creative minds in European history, as revealed in the list dated 1956 contained within the Dossiers Secrets and listed in full under the entry in this book titled Grand Masters of the Priory of Sion. Many distinguished people held this position, including Leonardo Da Vinci, Isaac Newton, Victor Hugo, and Jean Cocteau, who is believed to have officiated from 1918 to 1963.

It's unclear exactly who became the Navigator of the Priory of Sion after Jean Cocteau's death in 1963, but the title eventually passed to Pierre Plantard, who served as the main public liaison for the society until his resignation in 1984.

During his term as Navigator, Plantard was the main source of information behind the international best-seller, Holy Blood, Holy Grail, having had direct contract with its authors as they were writing it. It was this book that brought the story of the Priory of Sion to the attention of the English-speaking world in 1982. In preparation for the book, coauthors

Michael Baigent, Richard Leigh, and Henry Lincoln spent years tracing and dissecting the genealogies, secret codes, and history of the secret society which were drip-fed to them via the strategic release of arcane documents and face-to-face interviews, which led them on a chase through the last 1,000 years of European history and political intrigue.

The trio never did ultimately discover what the real purpose of the Priory of Sion was. The restoration of a Merovingian monarch to the throne of France was high on Plantard's list of priorities, but so was the realization of an economic and political United States of Europe, which has now largely been achieved with the advent of the European Union and the implementation of the euro replacing the majority of local currencies.

Therefore, in the absence of any clear statement of purpose, Baigent, Leigh, and Lincoln themselves developed the revolutionary theory that the Merovingian bloodline might represent the vestiges of a lineage descending from the children of Jesus and Mary Magdalene (who, it is believed, found refuge in France after the Crucifixion) and that the purpose of the Priory of Sion was, in fact, to guard this sacred lineage. Despite the fact that Pierre Plantard himself never actually confirmed or denied this theory, dozens of books have been produced over the past 20 years to explore the possibility that the lineage of Jesus and Mary Magdalene has continued within the bloodlines of Europe's aristocratic families.

After Plantard's resignation as Navigator in 1984, the Priory of Sion went underground again, despite persistent rumors that it was continuing under a multitude of guises. These rumors have, in turn, spawned numerous fictitious chivalric orders, some claiming to be the "real" Priory of Sion.

On December 27, 2002, a communiqué was released on official PoS stationery announcing the public re-launch of the society, signed by Pierre Plantard's former private secretary, Gino Sandri, under the title of General Secretary, and a mysterious unnamed woman as the Navigator. However, many insiders regard this re-launch as a publicity stunt.

And so the existence of the Priory of Sion continues to be an elusive mystery, even today.

See also: Dossiers Secrets; Grand Masters of the Priory of Sion; Plantard, Pierre.

Pyramide Inversée

"A remarkable anti-structure . . . a symbolic use of technology . . . a piece of sculpture. It was meant as an object, but it is an object to transmit light." So wrote the panel of judges of the 1995 Benedictus Awards, where the Pyramide Inversée was a finalist. Designed and executed by the firm of Pei, Cobb, Freed, and Partners, the designers of the great glass pyramid entrance to the Louvre, the Pyramide Inversée is a remarkable monument of glass that is positioned at the Métro system entrance to the Louvre.

In *The Da Vinci Code*, it is the small upright pyramid at the base of the Pyramide Inversée that holds the final answer to the riddle posed in the book.

The Pyramid Inversée is a 30-ton, 43.6-foot-square steel and glass caisson frame in the shape of an upside-down pyramid pointing down into the underground chamber. It is all but invisible from above ground, being positioned within the grassed circular junction of the main access road through the Louvre grounds. At night, the glass Pyramide Inversée is beautifully lit and animated by a series of lights and mirrors, serving as a monumental chandelier.

See also: Louvre.

Rose Line

The mystical term for a solar meridian, as opposed to the officially recognized scientific "prime meridian." The term has also been used to refer to the alleged bloodline of Jesus and Mary Magdalene. This term was explained to Sophie Neveu by Leigh Teabing and Robert Langdon while they were at Château Villette. Locations visited in the novel fall on two different Rose Lines, one in Britain and the other in France. In Paris, the line runs through the Louvre and then the gnomon in the Church of St-Sulpice. When Robert Langdon and Sophie travel to Rosslyn Chapel, they believe they are on another line and that the chapel's name is an abbreviation of Rose Line.

In the Priory of Sion's codes, we are led to imagine the earth as a center point encircled by the 12 zodiac signs, in the same way that the zodiacal houses encircle the ecliptic of the earth in space. A rather complex series of instructions or codes follows, eventually revealing that a fixed north–south line is constructed, called the Rose Line, with this fixed template being both a navigational map and a solar calendar.

It is this principle that underlies the famous solar meridian, or gnomon, at St-Sulpice in Paris, where Silas was sent to look for the keystone. At St-Sulpice, a beam of sunlight is focused through a lens in the southern transept window of the church at noon, and the movement of the earth around the sun is tracked throughout the year as the sunbeam moves along a brass strip, punctuated by plaques, across the floor of the church until it culminates at a marble obelisk in the north transept on the winter solstice (see St-Sulpice).

The idea of a compass rose was developed as a navigational aid, with the main arms of this rose marking the north, south, east, and west cardinal directions, with smaller arms marking the incremental directions in between. The northern position of the compass rose is traditionally designated by the fleur-de-lis symbol, which is also used as a heraldic symbol to denote royalty. In medieval times, the northern direction was also known as Septentriones, after the seven stars of Ursa Major, or the Great Bear, which acts as a pointer guide to the polestar. Hence, the bear symbolism is deployed in both Arthurian Grail

mythology and in Priory of Sion codes as a "guardian" symbol, and one of the names of the polestar, Stella Maris, or Star of the Sea, is attributed to Our Lady, or Notre Dame.

Therefore, perhaps it is no coincidence that the path of the Rose Line that bisects France from Dunkirk in the north, through Amiens, St-Sulpice in Paris, Bourges in the epicenter, through Carcassonne, terminating in Barcelona in Spain in the south is marked by an intriguing mixture of Notre-Dame cathedrals and churches with solar meridiana.

These same concepts are incorporated into a cryptic Priory of Sion poem titled "Le Serpent Rouge," or the Red Serpent, which encodes clues about how the solar meridian was incorporated into the fabric of the Church of St-Sulpice in Paris.

In the late seventeenth century, the invention of new scientific instruments and techniques enabled astronomers to calculate a much more accurate prime meridian, and the

135

ancient "organic" methods were abandoned. To this end, the Paris Observatory was completed in 1672 to mark the location of the new Paris zero meridian, which rendered the solar gnomon at St-Sulpice redundant.

Finally, in 1884, the world powers voted to move the earth's prime meridian to Greenwich in England, but the Rose Line lives on in the hearts of the followers of esoteric curiosities.

See also: Gnomon at St-Sulpice; Priory of Sion; St-Sulpice.

Rosslyn Chapel

The last site on Sophie Neveu's journey to discover the truth about her family, suggested by the last poem of Jacques Saunière: "The Holy Grail 'neath ancient Roslin waits..." She and Langdon travel to Scotland, where Sophie makes a wonderful discovery.

Contrary to popular opinion, Rosslyn Chapel was not built by the Knights Templar. The Poor Knights of the Temple of Solomon actually have no connection to Rosslyn Chapel whatsoever. The chapel was founded and paid for by Sir William St Clair, Earl of Rosslyn and Orkney, in the fifteenth century. The Templar order was destroyed over 100 years before the first stone of Rosslyn Chapel was laid. The only link between Rosslyn and the Templars was the fact that the Templar headquarters in Scotland had been a few miles from Rosslyn Castle and that the St Clair family testified against the Knights Templar when the members of the military order were brought to trial at Holyrood in Edinburgh in 1309.

Rosslyn Chapel lies a few miles south of Edinburgh in the small village of Roslin. Roslin itself hit the headlines as the birthplace of Dolly the sheep, which was cloned at the Roslin Institute. The chapel is a world-famous heritage building that has inspired artists and writers including Robert Burns, Sir Walter Scott, and William Wordsworth. It is also a working church with an active congregation and weekly services.

The chapel that stands today is a fraction of the full-scale cathedral that was originally planned. The correct name for the chapel is "the Collegiate College of St Matthew" and it is thought that the St Clair family, who founded the chapel, envisioned Rosslyn becoming a center for learning on a grand scale. Rosslyn Castle was home to a medieval scriptorium, where books from Continental Europe were translated and copied by hand. In many ways the carvings within the chapel mimic the intricate illuminations of medieval books of hours and bestiaries. Fabulous creatures such as dragons, unicorns, green men, lions, and monkeys rub shoulders with saints, knights, kings, queens, and a host of medieval musicians and biblical characters.

Roslin is not the original spelling of Rosslyn, and the name "Rosslyn" does not come from "Rose Line," contrary to the claims in The Da Vinci Code. It is in fact simply a name constructed from two Scottish words: "ross," meaning "hill," and "lynn," meaning "water." Rosslyn is literally the hill by the water. This name suits the place perfectly, as the River Esk bends around a large hill, which is the bedrock of Rosslyn Castle.

Over the past few years there have been a series of alternative history books that feature ever-more-fanciful theories regarding Rosslyn. It has been alleged that the Lost Ark of the Covenant, the Holy Grail, the secret Lost Gospels of Christ, the Knights Templars' treasure, and the embalmed head of Jesus are buried somewhere under the chapel. Some authors claim that the chapel has encoded within it the secret teachings of the Templars and the origins of Freemasonry. Locals have commented that they half expect someone to claim that the Loch Ness Monster and the Roswell UFO are hidden under the chapel too! There is a local legend about a vast treasure hidden at Rosslyn, but this tale is linked to the castle and not the chapel. The treasure is said to be worth many millions of dollars and is guarded by a dark knight and a ghostly white lady.

There is, however, a hidden chamber beneath Rosslyn Chapel. This crypt is the burial vault of the St Clair family. Generations of these Scottish knights lie buried in full suits of armor. The entrance to this tomb is well recorded and lies beneath stone slabs in the floor of the north aisle of the chapel. Excavations of the crypt have not been allowed, as Rosslyn is a working church and a delicate building that has already suffered from centuries of neglect. There is no hard evidence for any "secret treasure" hidden beneath Rosslyn. Any invasive excavation would only serve to damage the chapel.

Is there a magical line between Rosslyn and Glastonbury, as stated in *The Da Vinci Code*? Anyone with a ruler can draw a straight line between two points. The main structures that would fall on that line are the M5 and M6 motorways. Within the chapel, you will not find a Star of David-shaped pathway worn into the floor; this is a wholly fictional addition. Any sacred geometry within the chapel is based not on Solomon's Temple or "Templar masonry" but on the east choir of Glasgow Cathedral, which Rosslyn's architectural structure closely mimics. You will not find the two pillars "Boaz" and "Jachin" at Rosslyn. There are, however, three main pillars, including the famous Apprentice Pillar. Legend says that this pillar was carved by a young apprentice following a vision of a wondrous pillar he saw in a dream. The master mason, who had traveled to study in Rome, was so enraged and envious that he struck the apprentice and killed him.

There are hundreds of strange cubes with unusual carvings on each surface of the chapel, but cryptographers have been looking at them for only a few years. The "code" may or may not be factual. Deciphering any code would not reveal the entrance to the vault beneath Rosslyn Chapel, as that entrance is already well known. One theory is that the cubes' carvings somehow symbolize musical notes from a medieval song, as each arch of cubes ends with a stone angel playing fifteenth-century instruments.

The St-Clair name within the Priory of Sion Dossiers Secrets appears to have become connected with the St Clairs of Rosslyn only with the publication of *Holy Blood, Holy Grail*. "Marie" De St-Clair is entirely fictional, a fake name within the Priory's foundation documents. She does not exist in the historical record.

Rosslyn Chapel is a magical place. It is a treasure house of medieval imagery, which gives us a unique insight into the minds of scholars, lords, and artisans of the Middle Ages. The St Clairs of Rosslyn were Scottish nobles who fought alongside William Wallace and King Robert the Bruce. They became a wealthy and influential family within the Scottish court and ambassadors to France. Rosslyn Chapel was built at the height of their power as a house fit for God, filled to overflowing with wonders whose meanings have become lost over time.

See also: Dossiers Secrets; Knights Templar; Priory of Sion.

Sacred Geometry

The art of passing on divine wisdom through the use of geometric forms as symbols. Sacred geometry is an art form that has been utilized over the centuries, almost as a private language between initiates and those in the know. Sacred geometry was considered to be beyond the comprehension of mortal man, being an approximation of the sacred and profane.

This secret language has been used for millennia and was especially favored by the Greek philosophers and mathematicians, notably Plato and Pythagoras. Most of Plato's dialog, *The Timaeus*, is dedicated to a treatise on sacred geometry, and his description of the mythical island of Atlantis seems to show a use of sacred geometry and symbolism that is inherent within the story. The ancient Greeks actually assigned values and attributes to the so-called Platonic solids, investing them with meaning, and defining within this meaning their relationship to the divine and the world beyond.

A classic example of sacred geometry in use is the Cabala, a religious and philosophical system that claims insight into the divine. Cabala is a Hebrew word meaning "receiving" and it was originally said to have been "received" by a select few, a kind of hidden or secret language known only to initiates.

The idea of sacred geometry crops up throughout *The Da Vinci Code*, whether in the context of Langdon telling Sophie about Solomon's Temple, which was built using knowledge of sacred geometry, or Jacques Saunière arranging his dying body into the shape of a pentagram, an ancient divine symbol. As a "symbologist," Langdon is an expert in the subject.

See also: Fibonacci Sequence; Golden Ratio; Golden Rectangle; Pentagram.

Saunière, Jacques

The curator of the Louvre museum and secret Grand Master of the Priory of Sion, whose murder sent Robert Langdon and Sophie Neveu on a frantic quest to decode the clues he left in order to discover the Priory's secret before Opus Dei did.

Saunière's name is inspired by the well-known Priory of Sion mystery surrounding an enigmatic priest named Bérenger Saunière, who took up his new post at the church of St Mary Magdalene in the tiny village of Rennes-le-Château, France, in June 1885.

For the first six years of his ministry, the young and handsome Saunière lived a simple life in his poor backwater parish, hunting and fishing and immersing himself in the fascinating history of the area, which was introduced to him by Abbé Henri Boudet, the priest of the nearby village of Rennes-les-Bains. At this time, Saunière also employed a young peasant girl, Marie Derarnaud, as his housekeeper, who soon became devoted to him and later inherited his estate and his secrets.

In 1891, inspired by Boudet's romantic tales of local history, Saunière raised the funds to carry out a modest restoration of his church, which had been built in 1059 on the ruins of an earlier sixth-century Visigothic edifice. It is said that during Saunière's renovations of the altar, he found four ancient parchments concealed in the Visigothic pillars that supported the altar stone. No one has actually seen these mysterious parchments, but two are said to have been genealogies dating from 1244 and 1644 and two are said to have been encoded documents composed in the 1780s by Abbé Antoine Bigou, one of Saunière's predecessors at the church of St Mary Magdalene.

When the documents were decoded, they revealed even more cryptic messages. It is believed that Saunière, suspecting he had stumbled across something significant, consulted the bishop of Carcassonne, who immediately arranged for the young priest to take the parchments to Abbé Bieil and Emile Hoffet at the Seminary of St-Sulpice in Paris for examination and analysis. During his stay in Paris, it is said that Saunière visited the Louvre to purchase reproductions of paintings by Teniers and Poussin, two artists referred to in the decoded parchment messages.

On Saunière's return to Rennes-le-Château, his behavior became increasingly odd. At first he continued his church renovations, unearthing flagstones and defacing inscriptions on gravestones in the process. But then, accompanied by Marie Derarnaud, he began to go for long walks in the countryside, amassing a large collection of apparently worthless piles of rocks. Soon after that, he began to conduct a voluminous correspondence all over Europe and opened bank accounts in strategic locations in the south of France.

Then, in 1896, Saunière began to spend vast sums of money, embarking on a massive restoration and cryptically symbolic redecoration of the church of St Mary Magdalene, building a new road and water storage facilities for the village, and constructing a private manor house called Villa Bethania, which he never actually occupied. The grounds of the villa were elaborately landscaped featuring a glorious crenellated tower, christened the Tour Magdala, which was built into the side of the mountain, affording panoramic views across the valley. It is estimated that this so-called impoverished parish priest spent the equivalent of several million dollars over the course of the 20 years leading up to his death in 1917.

Predictably, Saunière's extravagant expenditure attracted the attention of the local ecclesiastical authorities, who called on him to explain the source of his immense wealth. When Saunière refused to account for his good fortune, the bishop accused him of illicitly selling Masses and a tribunal suspended him from his post. In response, Saunière appealed directly to the Vatican, which overruled the suspension and reinstated him.

Then, on January 17, 1917, Saunière suffered a massive stroke from which he never recovered. The date of Saunière's stroke is notable for its significance in Priory of Sion mythology as the Feast Day of St Sulpice, which, intriguingly, is also the date on one of the tombstones in his churchyard that Saunière had defaced.

It is said that the priest who attended Saunière to hear his last confession refused to administer the rite of extreme unction and that Saunière died unshriven on January 22.

Villa Bethania is cited in the Dossiers Secrets as the "arch," or mother house, of the 27 commandaries of the Priory of Sion sprinkled throughout France. Furthermore, Pierre Plantard, Grand Master of the Priory of Sion, has hinted that Rennes-le-Château is the location of a secret cache of Priory archives, and this rumor was underscored by the fact that Plantard himself had personally purchased property in the area.

Speculation about what Saunière might have discovered to make him a wealthy man continues over 100 years later, and treasure hunters comb the countryside to this day. But nothing of any significance has ever been found, and the mystery lives on.

See also: Plantard, Pierre; Priory of Sion; St-Sulpice.

Shekinah

This is included in lectures given by Robert Langdon, a professor in the novel, as part of a study of the role of sex as a pathway to God. He is trying to help Sophie Neveu come to terms with a ritual she had seen her grandfather participate in.

In the Targum, the Aramaic translation of the Bible, this term is used to indicate the manifestation of the presence of God among people. However, it seems that medieval Jewish scholars and philosophers, in order to avoid confusion and an anthropomorphic interpretation of this concept—which came about because of certain uses of the word in the Talmud and Midrash, where it is clear that the concept cannot be identical with God—introduced a separate female identity and existence for the Shekinah, though its role was only a minor one.

This separate identity in turn led to its use, within certain Cabalistic works and systems, as meaning "a consort of God," with much more importance and significance being placed on the concept. In the Cabalistic approach, the Shekinah can be reunited with God only through a fulfillment of all the divine commandments—so signaling the new messianic age.

See also: Langdon, Robert; Neveu, Sophie.

Silas

A member of Opus Dei, this character sincerely believes that he is performing the work of God as he wreaks havoc through *The Da Vinci Code*. He takes part in corporal mortification through wearing a cilice belt and by scourging himself. His name does not seem to have any hidden meaning; however, it may be a reflection of St Silas, a companion of St Paul, who is mentioned in Acts 15: 22 as one of the "leading men among the brethren."

See also: Cilice Belt; Opus Dei.

Solomon's Temple

In the book, Langdon tells Sophie that Rosslyn Chapel is a replica of Solomon's Temple.

According to Jewish and Christian tradition and teachings, King Solomon was the son of King David who went on to build a legendary temple on the summit of Mount Moriah in Jerusalem. As successor to King David, Solomon reigned over the kingdom of Israel from approximately 970 to 930 BC. His mother was Bath-Sheba, and his reign is noted for a number of foreign alliances that he supposedly established, notably with both the Egyptians and the Phoenicians, while at the same time building the nation of Israel into a formidable force and extending its boundaries and territory. Biblical sources state that his reign was marked by unrest in the north of Israel and by a revolt led by Jeroboam I. Most of what we know about Solomon is derived from II Samuel and I and II Kings in the Bible, as well as a small number of non-biblical sources, but what is strange is that it is nearly impossible to corroborate these stories about the king from the contemporary archaeological record. Solomon was fabled for his wisdom, and several books in the Old Testament are traditionally ascribed to his hand, notably the Song of Solomon. In the Koran, Solomon is known as Sulayman and is revered as a primary prophet within Islam.

Biblical tradition states that King David provided the building materials needed for Solomon's temple before his death, with Solomon adding substantially to the materials and plans later.

In the Bible, I Kings tells most of the story concerning the preparation of the temple site, with a huge wall being raised across the hill of Moriah and a massive leveling of the site being undertaken. Solomon is also accredited with the building of vast cisterns and channels in order to bring water to the site. The dimensions and architectural layout of the temple are relayed in detail in the Bible and have been the source of much debate and argument over the centuries concerning its true proportions and meaning. The temple was constructed to house the holy of holies, a place sacrosanct in the Jewish tradition and designed to hold the legendary Ark of the Covenant: the relic, or chest, that held the stone tablets of the Ten Commandments, the covenant between God and the Israelites. The Ark was a gold-plated chest that had on it images of the four Cherubim and was carried by two poles on either side of it. The Ark was the source of legendary power to the Israelites and has been written about ever since.

Before the temple entrance stood the two bronze pillars, Jachin and Boaz. These two pillars have also been the subject of much speculation and theory through the ages, and they play an important role in the traditions of modern-day Freemasons, who believe that their ancient craft and organization can be dated back to the building of the temple.

Freemasons revere the figure of Hiram Abiff, another name for Hiram I, King of Tyre, who entered into a strategic pact with King Solomon and who Freemasons believe assisted in the building of the temple.

Evidence of Solomon's reign and building regime is scant in today's Israel, leading many modern commentators to question whether Solomon actually existed. Some researchers point to the fact that his name seems to be made up of the words "sol" (sun) and "omon" (Amun, the Egyptian sun-god) and could in fact be a symbolic reference and wordplay.

Solomon's Temple is seen by traditionalists as an actual physical building, erected in the heart of ancient Jerusalem on Mount Moriah. However, with the lack of archaeological and corroborative evidence to back up this claim, many modern researchers and authors have come to a very different conclusion about Solomon, his life story, and his temple. Could the temple be symbolic of something else? A metaphor for a gateway to God? It has been postulated that many temples of Solomon existed around the ancient world and that in fact the measurements and dimensions given in the Bible are references to an esoteric sacred geometry. One researcher in Scotland, David Alan Ritchie, believes that he has identified a giant Solomon's temple built with massive landscape geometry on the ground in the Rosslyn Chapel area. It is even theorized by some that Rosslyn Chapel itself is styled on the plans for Solomon's Temple, with its ornate carvings and impressive pillars.

Whatever the truth, the fact remains that the idea of Solomon's Temple and what it represents has captured the attention of some of the greatest minds of the past several hundred years.

See also: Knights Templar; Rosslyn Chapel; Sacred Geometry.

St-Sulpice

The famous Parisian church where Silas was directed to look for the keystone at the bottom of the obelisk, beneath the Rose Line, by the top members of the Priory of Sion before they were murdered, as a diversionary tactic and prearranged distress signal.

The Church of St-Sulpice was built originally in the Merovingian era within the boundaries of the Abbey of St-Germain-des-Prés as a parish church for the peasants living within its domain on the Left Bank of Paris. The church is dedicated to St Sulpicius, the sixth-century Archbishop of Bourges whose Feast Day is January 17. Priory of Sion documents claim that the church was actually built on the remains of an earlier pagan Temple of Isis and that a statue of Isis was said to have been worshipped as the Virgin Mary at St-Germain until it was destroyed in 1514.

As the parish of St-Germain grew in importance due to the abbey's own church of St-Germain-des-Prés, which housed a piece of the True Cross and the tunic of St Vincent, St-Sulpice itself was continually rebuilt and enlarged to serve the growing local population, which was also becoming wealthier. Work on the current building, intended to serve the Seminary of St-Sulpice and to rival Notre-Dame de Paris in both size and importance, was begun in 1646, but immediately ran into financial difficulties. Six architects struggled to complete the project over a period of 134 years.

St-Sulpice is world renowned for its solar gnomon, a sundial system that tracks a beam of sunlight along a brass strip in the floor to mark the solstices and equinoxes. The sunbeam is designed to move across the breadth of the church from a hole in the south transept window and climb an obelisk in the north transept as the solar year progresses. In the Priory documents, the brass strip that marks the solar meridian is known as the Rose Line, which is also a pun on the story of St Roseline, who died on January 17, or alternatively as the Serpent Rouge (Red Serpent).

By special arrangement, the foundations of the original church of St-Sulpice can be seen in the crypt under the current church, but unfortunately the gnomon is now defunct, although the brass strip and the obelisk can still be seen.

Both Baudelaire and the Marquis de Sade were baptized in the church, and Victor Hugo was married here.

See also: Dossiers Secrets; Gnomon at St-Sulpice; Plantard, Pierre; Priory of Sion; Rose Line; Saunière, Jacques.

Sub Rosa

The sign used by Jacques Saunière to tell Sophie that he wanted privacy. Saunière used to hang a rose on his office door when he was having a confidential phone call and didn't want disturbing.

Sub rosa is an adjective meaning "secretive," "confidential," "private." It comes from the Latin, meaning "under the rose," and is associated with confidentiality because of the connection in ancient legend between the rose and secrecy. This in turn is from the classical story about Cupid giving the god of silence, Harpocrates, a rose in order to bribe him not to betray the confidence of Venus. In Roman banqueting rooms, the ceilings were often painted and decorated with roses to remind guests that whatever was spoken at the table was indeed sub rosa.

Teabing, Leigh

One of the main characters of *The Da Vinci Code*, Teabing lives in the splendid stately pile called Château Villette near Versailles. The name is actually an amalgam of part anagram, part straight name—with the authors Michael Baigent and Richard Leigh, two of the three writers of *Holy Blood, Holy Grail*, being honored. Teabing is an anagram of Baigent.

See also: Holy Blood, Holy Grail.

Temple Church

The place to which Langdon, Sophie, and Teabing are led by one of the clues in *The Da Vinci Code*, though this proves to be a false trail.

Located between Fleet Street and the River Thames, in London, England, Temple Church is a twelfth-century building. The church is still used today as a place of worship, with services on Sundays and visiting times from Wednesday to Sunday.

Temple Church was built by the Knights Templar, who before the current building was erected had met at a site in London's High Holborn area that had been established by Hughes de Payens, the first Grand Master of the order and one of the original nine Knights. Because the order was outgrowing this site, it was decided to purchase the land that the present site occupies and to build a much larger compound. This area originally contained not only the present church but also houses for the Knights, recreational grounds, and military training facilities. The junior members of the order, the novices, were not allowed to enter the City of London without the strict permission of the Master of the Temple.

Comprising two separate sections, the building is formed by the area known as the round church and an adjoining rectangular section known as the chancel. The chancel was added some 50 years after the building of the original round church.

The round church was based on the design of the Church of the Holy Sepulcher in Jerusalem, as were the traditions of the Templar order. The round church houses the first ever freestanding Purbeck marble columns that surround the 55-foot-diameter nave. The walls would originally have been painted in bright colors.

The round church was consecrated in 1185, on February 10, by Heraclius, Patriarch of Jerusalem. Some also speculate that Henry II, King of England, was also present at this ceremony. It is in the round church that some of the most interesting features of the building are found. As stated in *The Da Vinci Code*, the church is known for the marble effigies of nine Knights that are laid in the center of the round church floor. The main characters from the novel have come to look for "...a knight a Pope interred...", which is part of a clue they believe will lead them to the Holy Grail. The most famous of these Knights is William Marshal, who wanted to be buried as a Knight Templar, so was ordained into the order before his death. Marshal was knighted in 1167 and was a consummate jouster, winning tournaments around the country and being the victor in some 500 bouts—never losing one. Marshal was also instrumental in dealing with the rebellious barons, who made King John sign the Magna Carta (the "Great Charter" designed to curb the King's powers) at Runnymede in 1215, with Temple Church being an important site of negotiations. Indeed, Marshal was to become regent during the reign of King John's son, Henry III, who also expressed a desire to be buried in the church after his death.

Because of the wish of Henry to be buried in the church, it was decided to pull down the original choir and build a larger structure, now known as the chancel, which was consecrated in 1240, on Ascension Day. However, in the end all this was in vain, as Henry III altered his will to say he wanted to be buried in Westminster Abbey, though one of his infant sons who died very young is buried at Temple Church.

The Master of the Temple, as befits such a powerful order, sat in Parliament as the Primus Baro—the first baron of the realm. The Temple Church compound was used as a lodging place for Papal legates, kings, and dignitaries from all over Europe and as an early depository bank, holding the funds of nobles and knights of the realm who had entrusted their wealth with the order.

After 1307, when the Knights Templar were destroyed as an order, Edward II took control of the church and made it a Crown possession. Later, it was give to the Knights Hospitaller order, who in turn rented the Temple Church compound to two colleges of lawyers. These colleges were known collectively as the Inns of the Court and individually as the Inner and Middle Temples. They shared the use of the church and were granted its use in perpetuity by James I in 1608. To this present day they continue to do so.

Temple Church has seen many episodes of history unfold within its walls: from the negotiations that led to Magna Carta, the abolition of the Knights Templar, the battle of the pulpits in the 1580s between the Calvinists and the Church of England, a refurbishment by Sir Christopher Wren—who added an organ to the church for the first time—through to a German bombing raid in 1941, which set the roof of the round church ablaze and destroyed the organ and much of the Victorian restoration of the church. It was during this raid that the Purbeck marble columns in the nave were irreparably damaged, cracking during the intense heat, and subsequently being replaced. One interesting thing to note is that the original marble columns had a slight outward lean, which was replicated in the replacements. The church was rededicated in November 1958.

William Shakespeare, in his play *Henry IV, Part I*, depicts the plucking of two roses, in his scene describing the start of the Wars of the Roses, in the Temple garden. A series of white and red roses was planted in 2002 to commemorate this scene.

See also: Knights Templar.

Vitruvian Man

Vitruvius, the architect, says in his work on architecture that the measurements of the human body are distributed by nature as follows: that is that 4 fingers make 1 palm, and 4 palms make 1 foot, 6 palms make 1 cubit, 4 cubits make a man's height. And 4 cubits make one pace and 24 palms make a man; and these measures he used in his buildings. If you open your legs so much as to decrease your height 1/14 and spread and raise your arms until your middle fingers touch the level of the top of your head, you must know that the center of the outspread limbs will be in the navel and the space between the legs will be an equilateral triangle. The length of a man's outspread arms is equal to his height. From the roots of the hair to the bottom of the chin is the tenth of a man's height; from the bottom of the chin to the top of his head is one eighth of his height; from the top of the breast to the top of his head will be one sixth of a man. From the top of the breast to the roots of the hair will be the seventh part of the whole man. From the nipples to the top of the head will be the fourth part of a man. The greatest width of the shoulders contains in itself the fourth part of the man. From the elbow to the tip of the hand will be the fifth part of a man; and from the elbow to the angle of the armpit will be the eighth part of the man. The whole hand will be the tenth part of the man; the beginning of the genitals marks the middle of the man. The foot is the seventh part of the man. From the sole of the foot to below the knee will be the fourth part of the man. From below the knee to the beginning of the genitals will be the fourth part of the man. The distance from the bottom of the chin to the nose and from the roots of the hair to the eyebrows is, in each case, the same, and like the ear, a third of the face.

The preceding is the complete translation of the text accompanying Leonardo Da Vinci's *Vitruvian Man*. It is actually a translation of Vitruvius, as Leonardo's drawing was originally an illustration for a book on the works of Vitruvius.

The *Vitruvian Man* is probably one of Leonardo's most famous and recognizable images. In *The Da Vinci Code*, it is also Sophie Neveu's favorite Da Vinci work, and it is the pose in which her grandfather, Jacques Saunière, arranged his body before he died.

The image of the man with two pairs of outstretched arms and two pairs of outstretched legs has adorned postered walls for a couple of generations at least. Vitruvius was a Roman engineer, writer, and architect of the late first century BC and the early first century AD. His one extant book, *De Architectura*, contains 10 huge encyclopedic chapters in which he discusses aspects of Roman town planning, engineering, and architecture—but also includes a section on human proportions. His re-discovery and importance once again in the Renaissance fueled the growth of classicism during that period—and indeed in subsequent periods.

The composition of the *Vitruvian Man*, as illustrated by Leonardo Da Vinci, is based wholly on the treatise cited above, by Vitruvius, on the dimensions of the human body, which have been proved to be largely correct, the emphasis being on rationalization of the geometry, by means of small whole numbers, to build the composition.

See also: Leonardo Da Vinci; Neveu, Sophie; Saunière, Jacques.

BIBLIOGRAPHY

RECOMMENDED MAIN READING

Baigent, Michael; Leigh, Richard & Lincoln, Henry:
The Holy Blood and the Holy Grail* (Arrow, 1996)

Baigent, Michael; Leigh, Richard & Lincoln, Henry:
The Messianic Legacy (Arrow, 1996)

Baigent, Michael; Leigh, Richard & Lincoln, Henry:
The Temple and the Lodge (Arrow, 2000)

Baigent, Michael & Leigh, Richard: *The Elixir and the Stone: The Tradition of Magic and Alchemy* (Viking, 1997)

Greene, Liz: *The Dreamer of the Vine* (Bodley Head, 1980)

Lincoln, Henry: *The Holy Place: The Mystery of Rennes-le-Chateau*
(Weidenfeld & Nicolson Illustrated, 2002)

Picknett, Lynn & Prince, Clive: *The Templar Revelation: Secret Guardians of the True Identity of Christ* (Corgi, 1998)

Starbird, Margaret: *The Woman With the Alabaster Jar: Mary Magdalene and the Holy Grail* (Bear & Company, 1993)

Starbird, Margaret: *The Goddess in the Gospels: Reclaiming the Sacred Feminine* (Bear & Company, 1998)

Stoyanov, Yuri: *The Other God* (Yale University Press, 2000)

THE SACRED FEMININE AND THE GODDESS

Ashe, Geoffrey: *The Virgin: Mary's Cult and the Re-Emergence of the Goddess* (Arkana, 1988)

Begg, Ean: *The Cult of the Black Virgin* (Arkana, 1996)

Haskins, Susan: *Mary Magdalene, Myth and Metaphor* (Riverhead Books, 1995)

Kinstler, Clysta: *The Moon Under Her Feet: The Story of Mari Magdalene in the Service to the Great Mother* (HarperCollins, 1989)

Markale, Jean: *Courtly Love: The Path of Sexual Initiation* (Inner Traditions, 2000)

Pagels, Elaine: *The Gnostic Gospels* (Penguin, 1990)

Robinson, James M. (ed.): *The Nag Hammadi Library* (HarperCollins, 1990)

Stoyanov, Yuri: *The Hidden Tradition in Europe*
(Arkana, 1994)

*Published in the United States of America as *Holy Blood, Holy Grail* (Dell, 1983)

MYSTIC ARTS

Andrew, Christopher (ed.): *Codebreaking and Signals Intelligence* (Frank Cass, 1986)

Boulton, D'Arcy J.D.: *Knights of the Crown* (Palgrave Macmillan, 1987)

Burman, Edward: *The Templars, Knights of God* (Inner Traditions, 1990)

Cooper-Oakley, Isabel: *Masonry & Medieval Mysticism* (Theosophical Publishing House London, 1977)

Daraul, Arkon: *A History of Secret Societies* (Citadel Press, 1984)

Delaforge, Gaeton: *The Templar Tradition in the Age of Aquarius* (Threshold Books, 1987)

Fortune, Dion: *The Mystical Qabalah* (Weiser Books, 2000)

Godwin, Joscelyn (transl.): *The Chemical Wedding of Christian Rosenkreutz* (Phanes Press, 1994)

Hall, Manly P.: *Secret Teachings of All Ages* (Deep Books, 2003)

Highfield, A.C.: *The Book of Celestial Images* (Bargo Press, 1986)

Horne, Alexander: *King Solomon's Temple in the Masonic Tradition* (HarperCollins, 1972)

Jung, C.G.: *Mysterium Coniunctionis* (Princeton University Press, 1977)

Jung, C.G.: *Psychology and Alchemy* (Routledge, 1980)

Jung, C.G.: *On the Nature of the Psyche* (Routledge, 2001)

Kieckhefer, Richard: *Magic in the Middle Ages* (Cambridge University Press, 1989)

Knight, Gareth: *A Practical Guide to Qabalistic Symbolism* (Red Wheel/Weiser, 2002)

MacGregor Mathers, S.L. (transl.): *The Kabbalah Unveiled* (R A Kessinger, 1998)

Robinson, John J.: *Born in Blood: The Lost Secrets of Freemasonry* (M Evans & Co, 1999)

Robinson, John J.: *Dungeon, Fire, and Sword* (Caxton Editions, 2001)

Roob, Alexander: *Alchemy & Mysticism* (Taschen, 2001)

Runciman, Steven: *The Medieval Manichee* (Cambridge University Press, 1982)

Runciman, Steven: *A History of the Crusades* (Vols 1-3) (Penguin, 1991)

Stevenson, David: *The Origins of Freemasonry: Scotland's Century 1590-1710* (Cambridge University Press, 1980)

Waite, Arthur Edward: *The Hermetic Museum* (Red Wheel/Weiser, 1991)

Waite, Arthur Edward: *The Brotherhood of the Rosy Cross* (R A Kessinger, 1998)

Watson, William: *The Last of the Templars* (The Harvill Press, 1998)

Webster, Nesta H.: *Secret Societies and Subversive Movements* (G S G & Associates, 1972)

Wood, Ian: *The Merovingian Kingdoms 450-751* (Longman, 1993)

Yates, Frances A.: *The Art of Memory* (Pimlico, 1992)

CELESTIAL AND TERRESTRIAL CODES

Allen, Richard Hinckley: *Star Names, Their Lore and Meaning* (R A Kessinger, 2003)

De Santillana, Giorgio & Von Dechend, Hertha: *Hamlet's Mill: An Essay Investigating the Origins of Human Knowledge and Its Transmission Through Myth* (Harvard Common Press, 1969)

Heilbron, J.L.: *The Sun in the Church: Cathedrals as Solar Observatories* (Harvard University Press, 1999)

Michell, John: *The Dimensions of Paradise: The Proportions and Symbolic Numbers of Ancient Cosmology* (Adventures Unlimited, 2001)

Michell, John & Rhone, Christine: *Twelve-Tribe Nations and the Science of Enchanting the Landscape* (Phanes Press, 1991)

Richer, Jean: *Sacred Geography of the Ancient Greeks, Astrological Symbolism in Art, Architecture, and Landscape* (State University of New York Press, 1994)

Rigby, Greg: *On Earth As It Is in Heaven: Revelations of French Cathedral Locations* (Rhaedus Publications, 1996)

ARCHITECTURAL CODES

Charpentier, Louis: *The Mysteries of Chartres Cathedral* (A B Academic Publishers, 1997)

De Lubicz, Schwaller: *The Temple of Man, Vols I and II* (Inner Traditions, 1998)

Fulcanelli: *The Mystery of the Cathedrals* (Aims International Books, 1982)

Querido, Rene: *The Golden Age of Chartres: The Teachings of a Mystery School and the Eternal Feminine* (Floris Books, 1987)

ARTISTIC CODES

Cook, Theodore Andrea: *The Curves of Life* (Dover Publications, 1979)

Ghyka, Matila: *The Geometry and Art of Life* (Dover Publications, 1978)

Huntley, H.E.: *The Divine Proportion, A Study in Mathematical Beauty* (Dover Publications, 1970)

Lehner, Ernst: *Symbols, Signs, and Signets* (Dover Publications, 1969)

Poynder, Michael: *Pi in the Sky* (Collins Press, 1997)

MATHEMATICAL CODES

Borissavlievitch, M.: *The Golden Number* (Tiranti, 1958)

Colman, Samuel: *Nature's Harmonic Unity: A Treatise on its Relation to Proportional Form* (Arno Press, 1976)

Herz-Fischler, R.: *A Mathematical History of the Golden Number* (Dover Publications, 1998)

Runion, Garth E.: *The Golden Section* (Non Basic Stock Line, 1990)

Vajda, Steven: *Fibonacci and Lucas Numbers and the Golden Section: Theory and Application* (Ellis Horwood, 1989)

Wentworth Thompson, D'Arcy: *On Growth and Form* (Cambridge University Press, 1992)

THE HOLY GRAIL

Begg, Ean & Deike: *In Search of the Holy Grail and the Precious Blood* (HarperCollins, 1995)

Godwin, Malcolm: *The Holy Grail: Its Origins, Secrets & Meaning Revealed* (Penguin, 1994)

Goodrich, Norma Lorre: *The Holy Grail* (HarperPerennial, 1993)

Matthews, John: *The Elements of the Grail Tradition* (Element Books, 1996)

RENNES-LE-CHÂTEAU

Andrews, Richard & Schellenberger, Paul: *The Tomb of God* (Time Warner, 1997)

Byrne, Patrick: *Templar Gold* (Blue Dolphin Publishing, 2001)

Fanthorpe, Lionel & Patricia, and Wallace-Murphy, Tim: *Rennes-le-Château: Its Mysteries and Secrets* (Red Wheel/Weiser, 2004)

James, Stanley: *The Treasure Maps of Rennes-Le-Château* (Maxbow Publishing, 1984)

Markale, Jean: *The Templar Treasure at Gisors* (Inner Traditions, 2003)

Patton, Guy & Mackness, Robin: *Web of Gold* (Sidgwick & Jackson, 2000)

Putnam, Bill, & Wood, John Edwin: *The Treasure of Rennes-le-Château* (Sutton Publishing, 2003)

BIBLIOGRAPHY

Wood, David: *Genesis: The First Book of Revelations* (Baton Wicks Publications, 1985)

Wood, David & Campbell, Ian: *Geneset: Target Earth* (Bellevue Books, 1994)

ROSSLYN CHAPEL

Gerber, Pat: *The Search for the Stone of Destiny* (Canongate Books Ltd, 2000)

Green, James: *Rosslyn Chapel: The Enigma – The Myth* (Temple Arch Publishers, 2002)

Knight, Christopher & Lomas, Robert: *The Hiram Key* (Arrow, 1997)

Sinclair, Andrew: *The Sword and the Grail* (Birlinn Limited, 2002)

Wallace-Murphy, Tim & Hopkins, Marilyn: *Rosslyn: The Guardian of the Secrets of the Holy Grail* (Element Books, 1999)

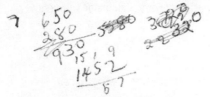

PICTURE CREDITS